KNIT
NORDIC

KNIT NORDIC

20 contemporary accessories inspired by 4 traditional sweater patterns

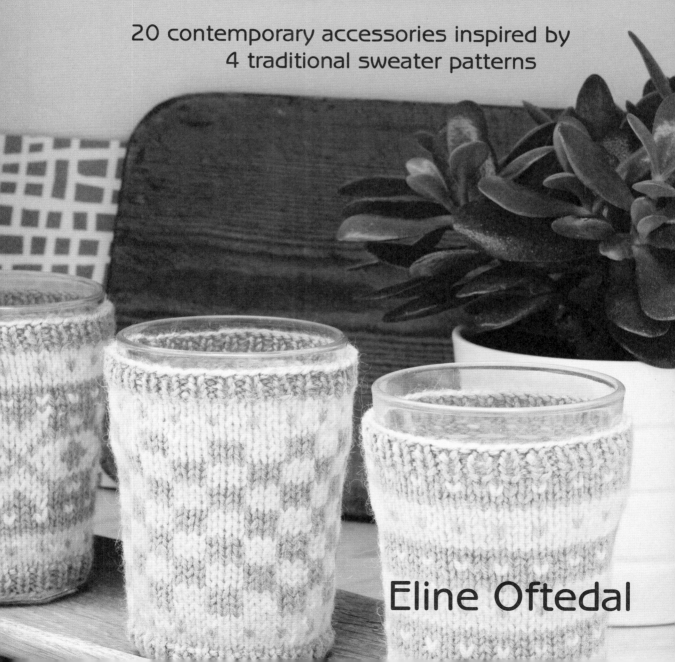

Eline Oftedal

CONTENTS

Fana

Voss

INTRODUCTION

If you are reading this book, you probably already like to knit, or are thinking that you would like to try it out. It's easy to see why you might want to make your own accessories and clothes – knitted garments and accessories are always in fashion! No catwalk or home interiors magazine is without knitted items, summer or winter. If you look closely at modern fashions you will often recognize traditional styles: fishermen's cable sweaters, geometrically patterned Norwegian styles and intricate, colourful Fair Isle patterns are perennial fashion favourites among designers.

The great thing about knitting is that you can easily make stylish designs yourself once you have mastered a few basic skills. It is a very portable hobby: you can knit wherever you are and it is easy to tuck your work in progress into a bag when you go out. For me, knitting has been a pleasant way to pass time in airports and spend evenings away from home. I have worked for many years in international politics and knitting has made all the travelling more bearable, although it's not as good as knitting snugly at home!

In times past, knitting was often an activity that brought a bit of extra income to a family. My grandmother used to handknit Marius sweaters for a Norwegian company, and my mother told me that she was sent out to pick up the yarn to bring home for her mother. My grandmother was not paid much, but it was a contribution to the family's income. In a continuation of knitting tradition, it was my mother who taught me to knit and my grandmother who taught me to crochet.

In this book you will find 20 projects inspired by four traditional Norwegian patterns: the Setesdal sweater, the Fana cardigan, the Marius ski sweater and the Voss cardigan. My inspiration for this book came from thinking that these classic garments were large and time-consuming projects to embark upon; sometimes you end up with a garment so warm that, with a bit of luck on the cold-weather front, you might only wear once a year.

This book offers you fresh ways to enjoy these design classics by reimagining them in new forms and shapes; you can keep your gadgets protected with the iPad and iPhone covers (pp. 40–43 and pp. 92–93), keep warm with an elegant beret or cosy wristwarmers (pp. 62–65 and pp. 52–55) or add a little Scandinavian style to your living room and kitchen with the cushion and potholders (pp. 88–91 and pp. 84–85).

The book not only offers knitting inspiration with its fresh twists on Norwegian designs, but there are also basic patterns here that you could easily adapt to other colourways. If you like a project but don't like the colours, just imagine it all in white and you have a clean slate to colour it the way you want to.

If, like me, you appreciate traditional Norwegian knitting and prefer modern, stylish accessories and household items, I am sure you will like the patterns in this book. I hope the book will inspire you to think of new forms and shapes to knit and to update traditional designs by applying them in fresh and original ways.

A taste of my Norway: blue tit chicks feeding at my summer house; a winter scene by Randsfjorden lake; lambs grazing in Lofoten.

KNITTING IN NORWAY

People have been knitting in Norway for centuries. Socks and undergarments, which need to have more flexibility than woven fabrics, were probably the first knitted items that were produced. Sweaters have probably been knitted since the early to mid-1700s. This book was inspired by four of the classic Norwegian patterns, but the history and heritage of our knitting tradition is much richer: if you want to learn more, I recommend the book *Everyday Knitting: Treasures from a Ragpie* by Annemor Sundbø.

Norway's distinctive sweater patterns have become known all over the world as a result of trade. The Norwegian word for 'sweater' is 'genser', which derives from the word 'gansey', the name of the traditional Guernsey fishermen's sweaters. Some of the patterns in this book have a long history, some have a shorter one, but they all have a fascinating heritage.

In the 1950s and 60s, knitted sweaters were at their most popular. Any school photo from that time shows all the pupils in handknitted sweaters.

Marius

Marius is the youngest of the patterns featured in this book; it first appeared in the 1950s, but traces its roots back to the Setesdal pattern. The birth of the Marius pattern is like a drama from the knitting world, with some handsome downhill skiers and an Olympic gold medal thrown in for good measure.

Handknit sweaters were the height of fashion in the postwar era, and many designers shared their creativity in knitting magazines and booklets published by yarn producers. Bitten Eriksen was a knitwear designer who created designs for a wool mill. She was also the mother of the well-known skiers Stein and Marius Eriksen; Stein won a gold medal at the Oslo Winter Olympics in 1952. The Marius pattern is a variety of the Setesdal pattern rendered in the Norwegian flag colours of red, white and blue, and Bitten's published designs, modelled by her famous sons, became very popular and sold well. Another knitwear designer, Unn Søyland Dale, happened to work for the Eriksens' sports store in Oslo; she sold a pattern very similar to the Marius design to a rival wool mill, thus triggering a dispute over property rights for what remains the most popular knitting pattern in Norway to this day. As the sweater was so heavily inspired by Setesdal, the pattern is regarded as common property, and officially neither woman is the mother of the Marius sweater. However, they both contributed to giving subsequent generations a classic sweater to love.

Traditional knitting patterns have always changed and developed throughout the years. It was in the 1930s that patterns became standardized through magazines and books from yarn producers. As knitters, we have always copied each other but often add a personal twist. I hope you will add your own personal twist to the patterns you knit from this book and hence become a little part of our knitting history.

The handsome downhill skier, actor and World War II hero Marius Eriksen helped to make the Marius sweater a must-have among young people in Norway. His sweater was knitted by his mother, Bitten Eriksen.

Setesdal

The Setesdal sweater originates from the Setesdal valley in the
southern part of Norway. The first documentation of the
sweater dates back to 1848, when the artist Adolph Tidemand
made a sketch of a young man wearing the sweater while
visiting the area. The sweater was, and still is, knitted in black
and white or grey and white, with a series of borders that the
knitter combines in different ways.

Traditionally, the Setesdal was a man's sweater. It was knitted
in the round from the bottom hem up to the neck, then the
armholes were cut into the knitting ('steeked'). The bottom
part was tucked into the trousers; because this part did not
show, it was often knitted in plain white yarn, which was
cheaper and more readily available than the darker-coloured
yarns. Cloth and woven fabrics had a higher standing than
knitted garments, so the best-wear sweaters had richly
embroidered fabric panels sewn on the cuffs and the neck
opening. The national costume from Setesdal often features
this beautiful sweater instead of a shirt.

In the 1930s, knitting patterns featuring the Setesdal design
started to appear in women's magazines, and this led to a
standardization of the pattern. It is likely that the patterns were
inspired by fishermen's sweaters from France and Guernsey
that were knitted in a single colour, with knit and purl stitches
making up the pattern. In the Setesdal sweater, the knits
and purls are knitted in colours. The closest town to Setesdal
is the port city of Kristiansand, and it is possible that a knitter
had seen a French fisherman's sweater at the harbour and
been inspired by the design; or maybe a young man went to
sea and came back with a foreign sweater. There is a striking
similarity between Fair Isle patterns and the Setesdal sweater
too; I often think of Setesdal as a black and white version of
Fair Isle sweaters.

No other Norwegian knitting pattern has inspired so many
knitters and designers for so long. Big designer names in
Europe and the United States still take inspiration from this
simple and beautiful pattern and reinvent it for the catwalk.

Fana

The Fana sweater originates from the Bergen region on the west coast of Norway. For centuries, Bergen was the main trading town in Norway, so foreign fashions came to Bergen first before spreading to the rest of the country.

The Fana sweater is made up of a striped pattern, with a star design at the top and a checked pattern at the hem. Photographs of fishermen wearing this sweater in Bergen date back to the late 1800s and early 1900s; in a painting by Adolph Tidemand from 1859, *Ship in Distress*, one of the crew is wearing a sweater that looks like the Fana pattern. The origins of the pattern before it reached Norway are not known, but seamen from the Baltic countries, the British Isles, the Low Countries, France and Germany all traded in Bergen, so local knitters could have taken inspiration from any of these. To my mind, Fana looks something like the traditional stripy sweaters that come from Brittany.

As with the Setesdal sweater, there are many varieties of the Fana sweater; some old cardigans feature fabric and ribbon embellishments. In the 1930s, Fana patterns started to become available commercially, and the design was standardized. This design enjoyed enormous popularity in the 1950 and 60s; looking at old school photos from the time, sometimes the entire class is wearing a Fana sweater!

Voss

The Voss sweater is a relatively new pattern in knitting, originating from north of Bergen on the west coast, but it has been around for centuries in embroidery. The traditional costume from Voss features lovely black embroidery on white fabric on women's headgear and blouses. The Voss design is geometrical and often includes squares with a pattern inside. This inspired the Norwegian Home Arts and Crafts Association to design a sweater based on the design in the 1930s. Looking at the Voss pattern, it is easy to imagine that it shares some heritage with the Sanquhar pattern from Scotland. The Baltic countries also have similar patterns, so they may all have inspired each other.

The Voss pattern has not enjoyed quite the same levels of popularity as Setesdal, Fana and Marius over the last decades, but I believe it will make a comeback, as nothing so beautiful will ever disappear.

In 1953, Princess Ragnhild (left) was engaged to be married to Erling Lorentzen (on skis). The media caught photos of the happy couple wearing Fana sweaters on the slopes. Another traditional sweater hit the fashion world!

Sakrisøy in Lofoten is an old Norwegian fishing hamlet. Today it is one of my favourite places to relax and catch a cod!

MARIUS

ALL-DAY HANDBAG

Most women need more than one bag, and this will be a great addition to your collection. Knitted handbags have a lovely informal look and can be very distinctive if knitted in bold patterns and colours. This bag is knitted in thick, chunky yarn, on slightly smaller needles than recommended for the yarn in order to achieve a firm, dense fabric. The main part and the lining are knitted in the round, while the base is knitted straight. You can either knit the handles or attach a ready-made pair bought from a craft store. Cut the canvas interfacing for the base of the bag after you have knitted it to get the right size.

You could knit a smaller version of the handbag using thinner yarn and smaller needles. Keep in mind that you will need to use wool yarn and opt for needles a size smaller than recommended on the yarn ball band to achieve a dense and sturdy fabric.

Size
Base 33 x 8cm (13 x 3¼in); height 26cm (10¼in)

Materials
Nine 50g balls in A (blue)
Two 50g balls in B (white)
One 50g ball in C (red)
Suggested yarn: chunky (bulky-weight) Shetland wool
60cm-long (24in) 6mm (US: 10) circular needle
Stitch marker
Two 6mm (US: 10) double-pointed needles for making i-cord (optional)
One pair of handbag handles (optional)
Piece of stiff plastic canvas for the base, 30 x 8cm (12 x 3¼in)
Tapestry needle
Sewing needle and thread

Tension
16 sts and 20 rows to 10cm (4in) square over st st using 6mm needles.

Pattern note
The outside, patterned part of the handbag and the inner, plain blue lining are knitted all in one piece; a purl row marks the border between the two and will form a ridge at the top of the bag. You will tuck the lining inside the bag, so you will have two knitted layers. This adds to the chunkiness of the bag. The base of the bag is knitted as a separate piece twice the length of the bag; this piece is folded in half, with a layer of plastic canvas placed in between to help the bag hold its shape, and then sewn into position.

Make the handbag
With yarn A, cast on 126 sts with circular needles. Join to work in the round, taking care not to twist the cast-on edge as you do so. Pm to mark beg of round.
Knit five rounds and then start working the chart (see p. 18). When you have finished round 48, purl one round in C.
Work 53 rounds in A, working every round as follows: K6, p2, k47, p2, k12, p2, k47, p2, k6 (the purl stitches will make up the corners of the handbag).
Check that the lining is the same length as the outside of the bag. Fold the lining inside the bag at the purl row to measure it. If the lining is too short, add rows to make it the same length as the outer part. The lining can be one row shorter than the outside of the bag, but should not be any longer.
Cast off loosely and weave in any loose ends.

Make the base of the handbag
With yarn A, cast on 16 sts. Work back and forth in garter stitch (knit every row) until the piece is 66cm (26in) long. Check that the base will fit neatly into the bag when it is doubled over; knit a few more rows or undo a few rows if necessary. Cast off and weave in any loose ends.

Chart for handbag

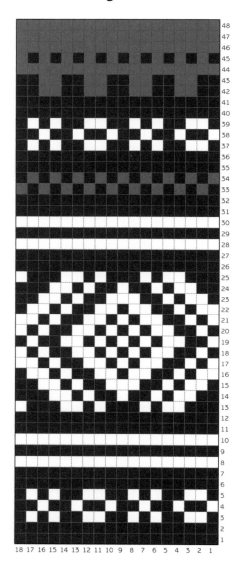

48 47 46 45 44 43 42 41 40 39 38 37 36 35 34 33 32 31 30 29 28 27 26 25 24 23 22 21 20 19 18 17 16 15 14 13 12 11 10 9 8 7 6 5 4 3 2 1

18 17 16 15 14 13 12 11 10 9 8 7 6 5 4 3 2 1

■ = A

☐ = B

■ = C

18-stitch pattern repeat (work 7 times)

Cut the plastic canvas to size and place it on one half of the base. Fold the knitted base double so the plastic canvas is sandwiched in between the knitted layers, then stitch the long edges together. Stitch the remaining short edge together and attach the base to the bottom of the handbag. Make sure you attach both layers (the outer part and the lining) at the same time. If it is difficult to reach both at the same time, stitch the outer part and the lining together before attaching the base. Stitch the handles in place (see below), tuck in your bare necessities and go for a walk in the park!

Options for making the handles
I chose to secure the ready-made wooden handles of the handbag with knitted cords, known as i-cords. If you would prefer to make knitted handles, I have included instructions for these too.

How to make i-cord
You will need two double-pointed needles to make i-cord. Knitting i-cord basically involves knitting in the round with two straight needles; this may sound confusing, but you will see what I mean as soon as you get going.
1 With yarn C, cast on 3 sts.
2 Slide the sts to the other end of the needle so that the working end of the yarn is on the left-hand side of the 3 sts rather than the right-hand side as normal.
3 With the other needle, pull the yarn around the back of the 3 sts and knit the sts.
Rep steps 2 and 3 until your i-cord is the length you want.
To finish, break the yarn 15–20cm (6–8in) from the work and thread the end through a tapestry needle. Pass the tapestry needle through the 3 sts and secure the end with a slipknot in the last of the 3 sts.

How to make knitted handles
Instead of buying handles for the handbag, you could knit them yourself. You could either make a single shoulder strap or two side handles in place of the wooden handles. Either way, try making the handles in moss stitch. This is made in a similar way to k1, p1 rib, but instead of placing the knit stitch of the live row over the knit stitch on the previous row (and the purls above the purls), for moss stitch you place the purl stitches over the knit stitches and vice versa. You will end up with quite a bumpy-looking, textured stitch that is strong and sturdy.

This is how to do it:

With yarn A and 6mm needles (you can use a pair of straight needles or the circular needle you used to knit the handbag), cast on 6 sts and work as follows:

Row 1: (K1, p1) to end of row.

Row 2: (P1, k1) to end of row.

Rep rows 1 and 2 until the handles or the shoulder strap are the desired length. Cast off in patt.

If you want thicker handles, you could make them over 12 sts and fold them double lengthways. With a tapestry needle, stitch up the long side with whip stitches.

With yarn A and a tapestry needle, stitch the handles or shoulder strap in place. After securing the thread, pass it into the bag and let it come out about 6–8cm (2¼–3¼in) away. Cut the thread close to the bag and pull the fabric taut so the yarn end disappears inside.

Inspirations

Have you ever seen a beautiful pattern on a garment but didn't want to buy it because you had no use for the coat or sweater it was on? This happens to me from time to time. Now that I always have a camera at hand (on my mobile phone), I take a photo and feel happy with that. This saves me a lot of money and space in my wardrobe! Sometimes I also draw up the pattern so I can knit it later. This way, I can apply the pattern to something I really want to use.

When you go to the shops, keep an eye out for patterns and colour combinations that you like. Take a photo and store it in an album you call 'inspirations'. Next time you want to knit something and find a pattern you like but not the colours, head to your inspirations folder and see if you can find a match between the item you want to knit and the patterns and colours you have saved. It might take a little longer to draw up your pattern and colours to fit the knitting pattern, but I can assure you that it is worth it!

Skill level
advanced

RACERBACK TOP

There is something sporty and sexy about a racerback. I believe that every fashion look can be re-created in knitting, and that belief inspired this design! You could wear the racerback top in many different ways; you could use it as a camisole with the matching hotpants on pp. 24–27 and head for bed, or slip it over a shirt and go to work. You could wear it under a cardigan or just as it is. I would opt for bed!

Sizes	Small	Medium	Large
Bust	83cm (32¾in)	90cm (35½in)	97cm (38¼in)
Length	50cm (19¾in)	51cm (20in)	53cm (21in)

Materials
Two[three:three] 50g balls in A (blue)
One[one:one] 50g ball in B (white)
One[one:one] 50g ball in C (red)
Suggested yarn: DK (worsted-weight) merino/alpaca blend
60cm-long (24in) 3.5mm (US: 4) circular needle
4mm (US: G6) crochet hook
Stitch marker
Five stitch holders (or scrap yarn)
Tapestry needle

Tension
26 sts and 28 rows to 10cm (4in) square over st st using 3.5mm needles.

Pattern note
The racerback top is knitted in the round from the bottom hem up to the armholes; the piece is then divided at the arm openings and worked back and forth in rows.

Make the top
With yarn A, cast on 216[232:252] sts. Join to work in the round, taking care not to twist the cast-on edge as you do so. Place marker to indicate the start of the round and work in k2, p2 rib until the piece measures 16[17:18]cm (6¼:6¾:7in).
Knit one round and inc 0[1:0] sts at each side.
(216[234:252] sts)
Knit 5[5:8] rounds and then start working the chart (see p. 23).
Note that for size M you should start at st 10. Start at st 1 for sizes S and L.
Start decreasing for the arm openings at round 29 of the chart as indicated.
Cont to dec as follows:
Cast off 6[7:8] sts, work chart for 96[103:110] sts, cast off 16[18:20] sts, work chart for 88[95:102] sts, cast off 10[11:12] sts.
Place the last 88[95:102] sts on a stitch holder for the back and cont working the front.

Make the front

With 96[103:110] sts, cont following the patt in the chart and dec 1 st at each side ten times as follows:

On RS rows: K1, k2tog, k to last 3 sts, k2tog, k1.
On WS rows: P1, p2tog, p to last 3 sts, p2tog, p1.

You will end up with 76[83:90] sts. End on a WS row.

Divide for the V-neck

K1, k2tog, k34[38:41], dec 2[1:2] sts, k34[38:41], k2tog, k1. (72[80:86] sts)

Place the 36[40:43] sts on the left side on a stitch holder and work the 36[40:43] sts on the right-hand side only. Start with a WS row at the V-neck edge and p1, p2tog and p to end of row.

Row 1: K1, k2tog, k to last 3 sts, k2tog, k1.
Row 2: P1, p2tog, p to end of row.

Rep these two rows until you have 8 sts left on the needle. Note that you continue with yarn C once you have completed the chart. Cont in C over the 8 sts until the strap measures 17[19:21]cm (6¾:7½:8¼in) from row 56.

Place the 8 sts on a stitch holder, and work the left-hand side the same way.

Make the back

With 88[95:102] sts (from stitch holder for back), knit one row with RS facing, following the pattern of the chart (knit on RS, purl on WS and work pattern on both sides).

Cast off 8 sts at beg of next four rows. (56[63:70] sts)

Dec 1 st at beg and end of next twelve rows. (32[39:46] sts)

Note that you continue with yarn C once you have completed the chart.

Cont over these sts until the work measures 44[45:47]cm (17¼:17¾:18½in) from the cast-on edge, ending with a WS row.

Divide the work for the shoulder straps

K12, cast off 8[15:22] sts, k12.

Place the 12 sts of one side on a stitch holder, and work the other strap.

Starting from the armhole side on the RS, k10, k2tog, k1. Purl one row.

Rep these two rows three more times until you have 8 sts left on the needle.

Place the sts on a stitch holder, and work the other strap in the same way.

Graft the straps together using Kitchener stitch (see p. 102). Weave in any loose ends.

With yarn C and 4mm crochet hook, crochet around the arm opening (see p. 104). Make sure you don't work too tightly or too loosely; you want to achieve a tension that defines the opening and is slightly tighter than the knitted edge. Do the same around the other arm opening and the front and back necklines. Weave in any loose ends.

With an iron set at a low temperature and using the steam function, gently press the straps flat. Do not press down too hard as it will leave the knitting looking flat and lifeless.

Now it's time to try the top on. How exciting!

Start the decrease for the arm opening here (row 29)

Chart for racerback top

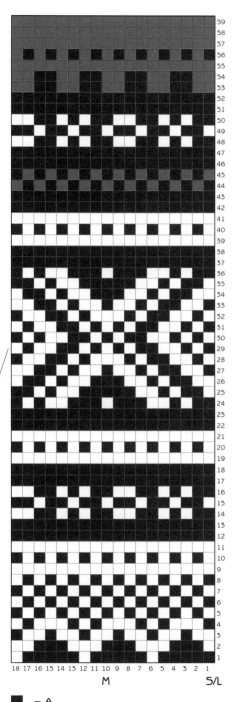

18 17 16 15 14 13 12 11 10 9 8 7 6 5 4 3 2 1

M   S/L

Start the pattern at the point indicated for the size you are making

■ = A

□ = B

■ = C

HOTPANTS

Knitted hotpants might not be what your grandmother would have knitted, but there's no reason why you can't! These hotpants will look great and feel cosy in bed or worn over a pair of tights at the weekend. You can combine them with the racerback top (pp. 20–23) to have a cool matching set. Knit the hotpants in an alpaca and silk blend yarn for a soft next-to-the-skin feel.

The hotpants are knitted from the bottom up on a circular needle. To shape the gusset, some of the knitting is done back and forth over the pattern. This might be a bit demanding if you are a fairly new knitter, but if you feel that these hotpants have your name on them, give it a try!

Sizes	Small	Medium	Large
Hips	86cm (34in)	100cm (39½in)	114cm (45in)
Leg width	49cm (19¼in)	56cm (22in)	63cm (24¾in)
Length	31cm (12¼in)	33cm (13in)	35cm (13¾in)

Materials

Three[three:four] 50g balls in A (blue)
One[one:two] 50g balls in B (white)
One[one:one] 50g ball in C (red)
Suggested yarn: 4ply (sport-weight) alpaca/silk blend
40cm-long (16in) and 60cm-long (24in) 3.5mm (US: 4) circular needles
Stitch marker
Stitch holder
Piece of ribbon for the drawstring waist, 100–110cm (39½–43¼in) long
Tapestry needle

Tension

26 sts and 28 rows to 10cm (4in) square over st st using 3.5mm needles.

Pattern note

You start by making one leg on the shorter circular needle, then set that leg to one side, make the second leg and then join the two legs together on the longer circular needle. You will need to join together the seam at the inside leg at the making up stage.

Make the hotpants

With yarn C and the shorter circular needle, loosely cast on 126[144:162] sts.
Join to work in the round, taking care not to twist the cast-on edge as you do so.
Place marker to indicate the start of the round.
Work six rounds in k2, p2 rib.
Start working the chart (see p. 26) and cont until round 28[28:35].
You will now start to decrease for the rise, continuing to follow the pattern as you work back and forth rows of in st st (knit on RS, purl on WS).
Note that you have to carry yarn A across on the WS on rows 37, 39, 47 and 49 as you need it on the same side as yarn B for the following rows.

Shape the crotch

Cast off 4[5:6] sts at beg of next two rows. (118[134:150] sts)
Dec 1 st (by working either k2tog or p2tog) at the start and end of every third[fourth:second] row, five[four:five] times. (108[126:140] sts)
Cont to work the chart back and forth until the work measures 17[18:20cm] (6¾:7:8in) from the cast-on edge.
Set the work aside on a stitch holder and work the other leg in the same way.

Join the legs

With the longer circular needle and, following the pattern of the chart, knit the sts from the first leg onto the needle and then the second leg, then place marker (this is the centre back). You now have 216[252:280] sts on the needle. Cont to work the pattern

Chart for hotpants

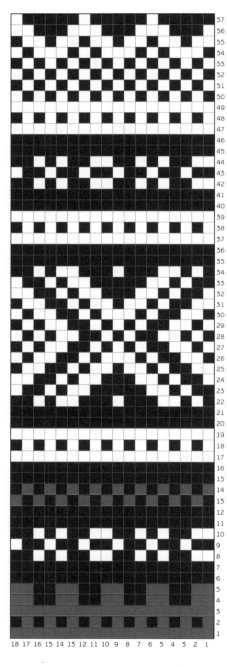

57
56
55
54
53
52
51
50
49 Carry yarn A along
48
47 Carry yarn A along
46
45
44
43
42
41
40
39 Carry yarn A along
38
37 Carry yarn A along
36
35 L: Start dec for crotch
34
33
32
31
30
29
28 S/M: Start dec for crotch
27
26
25
24
23
22
21
20
19
18
17
16
15
14
13
12
11
10
9
8
7
6
5
4
3
2
1

18 17 16 15 14 13 12 11 10 9 8 7 6 5 4 3 2 1

■ = A

□ = B

■ = C

18-stitch pattern repeat (work 7:8:9 times for each leg)

of the chart, working in the round. When you have finished the chart, cont with yarn A only, until the work measures 25[26:28cm] (10:10¼:11in) from cast on edge.

Shape the waist
Size Small only:
Next round: *K52, k2tog, rep from * to end of round. (212 sts)
Next round: K4, k2tog, *k9, k2tog, k9, rep from * to last 6 sts, k4, k2tog. (200 sts)
Next round: *K9, k2tog, k9, rep from * to end of round. (190 sts)
Work two rounds even.
Next round: *K29, k2tog, rep from * to last 4 sts, k to end of round. (184 sts)
Work two rounds even.

Size Medium only:
Next round: *K10, k2tog, k9, rep from * to end of round. (240 sts)
Work two rounds even.
Next round: *K10, k2tog, k8, rep from * to end of round. (228 sts)
Work three rounds even.

Size Large only:
Next round: *K54, k2tog, rep from * to end of round. (275 sts)
Next round: *K12, k2tog, k11, rep from * to end of round. (264 sts)
Work two rounds even.
Next round: *K11, k2tog, k11, rep from * to end of round. (253 sts)
Work two rounds even.
Next round: *K26, k2tog, rep from * to last st, k1. (244 sts)
Work four rounds even.

For all sizes:
K92[114:122] sts and move the stitch marker here to the centre front, k92[114:122] sts.
Work six[seven:seven] rounds in k2, p2 rib.
Eyelet round: *K2, p2, k2tog, yo, p2, rep from * to end of round.
Work five[six:six] rounds in k2, p2 rib.
Cast off in patt.

Finish the hotpants
Weave in any loose ends on the WS and sew up the inside leg seams. With an iron set on the 'wool' setting and using the steam function, carefully block the hotpants to shape. Starting at the front, weave the ribbon through the eyelet row. Then be brave and model the hotpants to show off your knitting skills!

MAURICE THE TEDDY BEAR

Everybody loves a teddy bear. Many adults still keep their childhood teddies somewhere, as we don't have the heart to throw away a threadbare friend! I am sure your old pal will not be jealous if you make Maurice. As the teddy bear is soft and has no parts that can come loose, he is perfect for babies and toddlers too.

Maurice is knitted from the bottom up in one piece using double-pointed needles. It can feel a bit fiddly to start with, but as this project is small you will progress quickly and never lose sight of the finish line. As you knit the teddy, you will need to stuff some fibrefill (toy stuffing) into his arms and legs before you get to the neck. It is easier to reach the extremities before the head is finished.

Size
27cm (10½in) tall

Materials
One 50g ball in A (blue)
One 50g ball in B (white)
One 50g ball in C (red)
Suggested yarn: DK (worsted-weight); most
 fibres will be suitable
Set of 3.5mm (US: 4) double-pointed
 needles
Stitch marker
Three stitch holders
Fibrefill (polyester toy stuffing)
Tapestry needle

Tension
22 sts and 27 rows to 10cm (4in) square
over st st using 3.5mm needles.

Pattern note
You start by working one of Maurice's feet in garter stitch; this is worked back and forth in rows rather than in the round. You then pick up stitches around the foot and work the leg in st st in the round. You make the whole of one leg first, then set the leg aside, make the second leg separately and then join the legs together to work the torso. When you make the arms, you start at the paw end and work up to the shoulder. Then you join the body and arms and work the neck and head.

Make the teddy bear
Make the legs
With yarn A, cast on 10 sts and work back and forth for 15 rows in garter stitch (knit every row). With a new knitting needle, pick up 10 sts from the left side of the square you just worked. Do the same for the right side with another needle and, with yet another needle, pick up 10 sts at the cast-on edge. You will now have four needles with 10 sts on each. (40 sts)
Place stitch marker to indicate the beginning of the round and work three rounds.

Start shaping the paw
Round 1: K19, k2tog, k8, sl1, k1, psso, k9. (38 sts)
Round 2: K18, k2tog, k8, sl1, k1, psso, k8. (36 sts)
Round 3: K17, k2tog, k8, sl1, k1, psso, k7. (34 sts)
Round 4: K16, k2tog, k2, sl1, k1, psso, k2tog, k2, sl1, k1, psso, k6. (30 sts)
Round 5: K15, k2tog, k1, sl1, k1, psso, k2tog, k1, sl1, k1, psso, k5. (26 sts)
Round 6: K14, k2tog, k4, sl1, k1, psso, k4. (24 sts)
K6 sts and place marker to indicate the centre back of the leg.
Distribute the sts so that you have 6 sts on each of the four needles.
Work 16 rounds.
Place the stitches on a stitch holder and work the other leg in the same way.

Join the legs and work the body

Start at the centre back of one of the legs and k6. Cast on 3 sts, k24 sts of the other leg and cast on 3 sts. Knit the rem 18 sts of the first leg. (54 sts)

Start working the chart for the body (see right) and cont until you have completed round 22 of the chart.

On round 23 dec for the arms as follows:
K12, cast off 2 sts, k26, cast off 2 sts, k12. (50 sts)

Place the stitches on a stitch holder and work the arms.

Make the arms

With yarn A, cast on 8 sts and move 4 sts onto another needle.

Work one round.

On the following rounds, inc as follows:

Round 1: K1, m1, k1, pm, k1, m1, k5. (10 sts)
Round 2: K2, m1, k2, m1, k6. (12 sts)
Round 3: K3, m1, k2, m1, k7. (14 sts)
Round 4: K4, m1, k2, m1, k8. (16 sts)
Round 5: K5, m1, k2, m1, k9. (18 sts)
Round 6: K6, m1, k2, m1, k10. (20 sts)

Distribute the sts evenly over four needles and work one round.

On the next round, dec as follows: *K3, k2tog, rep from * to end of round. (16 sts)

Work 15 rounds, start the chart for the arms (see opposite) and complete round 8.

At round 9, cast off the last 2 sts. (14 sts)

Place the stitches on a stitch holder and work the other arm in the same way.

Teddy bear body

Join arms and body (round 24)
Cast off for arms (round 23)

■ = A

□ = B

■ = C

18-stitch pattern repeat (work 3 times)

Join the body and arms

Start working at the centre of the teddy's back. K12 sts, k14 sts from the first arm, k26 sts across the front body, k14 sts from the second arm and the rem 12 sts of the back. (78 sts)

You have now completed round 24 of the body chart. Cont working the body chart. You will see that the pattern no longer adds up as you decrease for the shoulders and neck. Make sure the pattern is correct at the front and back and make the necessary adjustments at the shoulders.

Stuff the legs and arms at this point, as it will be more difficult when you have decreased for the neck.

Cont working the body chart, dec for shoulders as follows:

Round 25: K10, *sl1, k1, psso, k2tog, k10, sl1, k1, psso, k2tog*, k22, rep from * to *, k10. (70 sts)
Round 26: K9, *sl1, k1, psso, k2tog, k8, sl1, k1, psso, k2tog*, k20, rep from * to *, k9. (62 sts)
Round 27: K8, *sl1, k1, psso, k2tog, k6, sl1, k1, psso, k2tog*, k18, rep from * to *, k8. (54 sts)
Round 28: K7, *sl1, k1, psso, k2tog, k4, sl1, k1, psso, k2tog*, k16, rep from * to *, k7. (46 sts)
Round 29: K6, *sl1, k1, psso, k2tog, k2, sl1, k1, psso, k2tog*, k14, rep from * to *, k6. (38 sts)
Rounds 30 and 31: Knit.

Dec for the neck as follows:
Round 32: *K1, k2tog, rep from * to end of round. (26 sts)

Distribute the sts on the needles as follows:
Needle 1: 6 sts; needle 2: 7 sts; needle 3: 6 sts; needle 4: 7 sts.

Work one round (round 33).

Inc for the head:
Round 34: K6, m1, k1, m1, k12, m1, k1, m1, k6. (30 sts)
Round 35: K7, m1, k1, m1, k6, m1, k1, m1, k7, m1, k1, m1, k7. (36 sts)
Round 36: K8, m1, k1, m1, k18, m1, k1, m1, k8. (40 sts)

Inc for the nose as follows:
Round 37: K18, m1, k5, m1, k17. (42 sts)
Cont in yarn C only.
Round 38: K18, m1, k7, m1, k17. (44 sts)
Round 39: K18, m1, k9, m1, k17. (46 sts)
Rounds 40 and 41: Knit.
Round 42: K18, sl1, k1, psso, k7, k2tog, k17. (44 sts)
Round 43: K18, sl1, k1, psso, k5, k2tog, k17. (42 sts)

Teddy bear arms

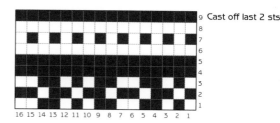

9 Cast off last 2 sts
8
7
6
5
4
3
2
1
16 15 14 13 12 11 10 9 8 7 6 5 4 3 2 1

■ = A

□ = B

Round 44: K18, sl1, k1, psso, k3, k2tog, k17. (40 sts)
Round 45: K18, sl1, k1, psso, k1, k2tog, k17. (38 sts)
Round 46: K18, sl1, k2tog, psso, k17. (36 sts)
Work seven more rounds, making sure you have 9 sts on
each needle.
Dec for crown as follows:
Round 1: *K7, sl1, k1, psso, k2tog*, k14, rep from * to * once, k7.
(32 sts)
Round 2: *K6, sl1, k1, psso, k2tog*, k12, rep from * to * once, k6.
(28 sts)
Round 3: *K5, sl1, k1, psso, k2tog*, k10, rep from * to * once, k5.
(24 sts)
Round 4: *K4, sl1, k1, psso, k2tog*, k8, rep from * to * once, k4.
(20 sts)
Cast off.

Make the ears
With yarn C, cast on 20 sts and distribute over four needles.
Work three rounds.
Inc as follows:
K4, m1, k2, m1, k8, m1, k2, m1, k4. (24 sts)
K one round.
Dec as follows:
Round 1: K4, *sl1, k1, psso, k2tog*, k8, rep from * to * once, k4.
(20 sts)
Round 2: K3, *sl1, k1, psso, k2tog*, k6, rep from * to * once, k3.
(16 sts)
Round 3: K2, *sl1, k1, psso, k2tog*, k4, rep from * to * once, k2.
(12 sts)
Round 4: K1, *sl1, k1, psso, k2tog*, k2, rep from * to * once, k1.
(8 sts)

Break the yarn about 20cm (8in) from the work. Thread the yarn
through the rem sts and pull tight. Pass the yarn through the middle of
the sts and secure the end on the inside of the ear. Make the other ear
in the same way.

Finish the teddy
Weave in any loose ends. Some can be hard to get to, but try to secure
them as best you can. Stuff the body and push the stuffing into the
arms and legs. When you feel the teddy is stuffed sufficiently, stitch up
the opening between the legs, under the arms and at the top of the
head. Stuff the ears and stitch in place where you think it gives your
teddy an expression you like. Using yarn A and a tapestry needle,
embroider the eyes, nose and mouth (see p. 105), referring to the
photograph as a guide. Secure the thread, pass it through the head and
cut off at the back. Pull the back of the head so that the thread
disappears on the inside.

Give your teddy a good hug!

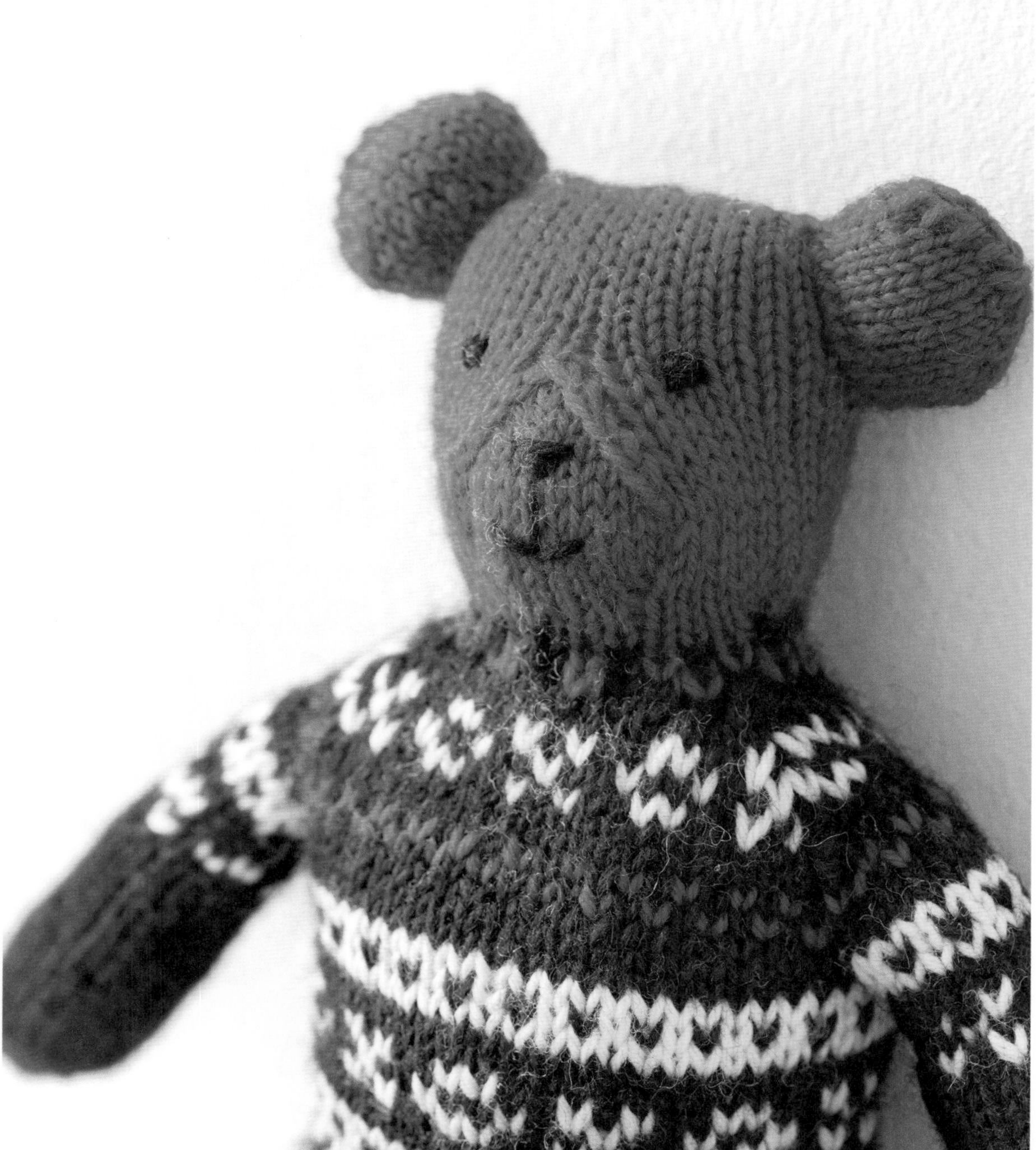

CHRISTMAS STOCKING

Everyone should have a Christmas stocking, regardless of their age. This one is big enough to hold lots of goodies and presents, so you never know what will happen when you hang it by the fireplace on Christmas Eve. The stocking is knitted from the top down on double-pointed needles. If you were wondering whether sock knitting is for you, this is a good project to try. If you discover you don't like it, there's no need to knit another one! The stocking is knitted with DK (worsted-weight) yarn held double; if you want to make a bigger and chunkier stocking, just use thicker yarn and larger needles.

Size
Top hem to toe 45cm (17¾in); circumference at top opening 38cm (15in)

Materials
Two 50g balls in A (blue)
Two 50g balls in B (white)
Two 50g balls in C (red)
Suggested yarn: DK (worsted-weight); most fibres will be suitable
Set of 4.5mm (US: 7) double-pointed needles
Stitch marker
Tapestry needle

Tension
Tension is not important for this project.

Pattern note
You start knitting from the top opening down to the heel and then down again to the toe. Work with the yarn held double.

Make the stocking
With yarn C held double, cast on 72 sts. Distribute the sts evenly over four needles (18 sts on each needle). Pm to mark beg of round.
Purl five rounds.
Start working the chart (see p. 36) in st st and work until you have completed round 48.

Heel
Turn the work and purl 36 sts in yarn B. Change to yarn C (held double) and work back and forth over the 36 sts as follows:
Row 1: Sl1, k35.
Row 2: Sl1, p35.
Rep these two rows three more times.

Turn the heel
Rows 1, 3, 5 and 7: Sl1, k to end of row.
Row 2: Sl1, p10, p2tog, p10, p2tog, p11.
Row 4: Sl1, p9, p2tog, p10, p2tog, p10.
Row 6: Sl1 p8, p2tog, p10, p2tog, p9.
Row 8: Sl1, p7, p2tog, p10, p2tog, p8. (28 sts)
Row 9: Sl1, k to end of row.
Row 10: Sl1, p6, p2tog, p10, p2tog, turn.
Row 11: Sl1, k10, turn.
Row 12: Sl1, p10, p2tog, turn.
Row 13: Sl1, k10, k2tog.
Rep rows 12 and 13 until all sts have been worked. End with a knit row. (12 sts)
Break the yarn.
With yarn B held double, pick up 12 sts along the side of the heel, knit the 36 sts that were left unworked while you made the heel and pick up 12 sts along the other side of the heel. (72 sts)

As you pick up sts, you can twist them to avoid creating holes. Place marker and distribute the sts evenly over the four needles (18 sts on each needle). The marker should be under the foot.

Cont to work the chart at round 50. When you have finished the chart, work in yarn A (held double) for 13cm (5in). Break the yarn.

Toe

Change to yarn C (held double) and dec for the toe as follows:

Round 1: *K6, k2tog, rep from * to end of round. (63 sts)
Rounds 2, 4, 6, 8, 10 and 12: Work even.
Round 3: *K5, k2tog, rep from * to end of round. (54 sts)
Round 5: *K4, k2tog, rep from * to end of round. (45 sts)
Round 7: *K3, k2tog, rep from * to end of round. (36 sts)
Round 9: *K2, k2tog, rep from * to end of round. (27 sts)
Round 11: *K1, k2tog, rep from * to end of round. (18 sts)
Round 13: *K2tog, rep from * to the end of round. (9 sts)
Break the yarn about 20cm (8in) from the work. With a tapestry needle, pass the thread through the rem sts and pull tight. Pass the thread through the middle of the sts and secure on the WS. If you feel that the stitches along the gusset are too big, take some yarn and weave into the sts from the WS and pull tight. Keep an eye on the RS to make sure it looks okay. Weave in any loose ends.

Make the hanging loop

With yarn C and holding the yarn triple, finger crochet a 10cm-long (4in) string (see p. 104). Stitch it in place at the back of the top of the stocking.
With an iron set on the 'wool' setting and using the steam function, carefully block the stocking to shape.

Hang the Christmas stocking by the fireplace and wait for Santa Claus to drop by!

Christmas traditions

In Norway and the Nordic countries, Christmas celebrations start on Christmas Eve. At 5pm, church bells can be heard all over the country, and Christmas has begun.

Chart for Christmas stocking

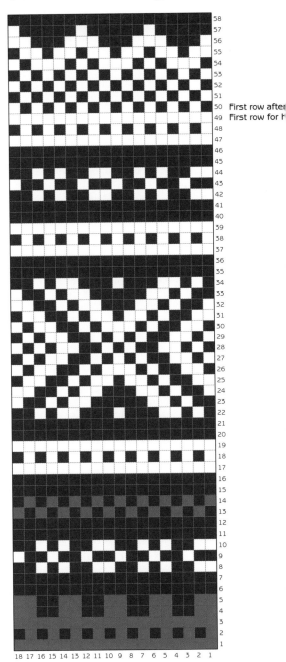

First row after
First row for H

18 17 16 15 14 13 12 11 10 9 8 7 6 5 4 3 2 1

■ = A
□ = B
■ = C

18-stitch pattern repeat (work 4 times)

SETESDAL

IPAD COVER

A knitted cover for your iPad will not only protect it, it will personalize it too. The classic Setesdal pattern has been used by designers for decades, and it's easy to see why. The intricate pattern is simplified by the monochrome black and white, but the design looks great in other colour combinations too.

This cover is lined inside to give extra protection to your iPad and to stop it from getting stuck in the long strands of yarn that occur on the wrong side of the knitting when working with two or more colours. The cover is knitted on a circular needle and cast off using the three-needle method. This is a quick knit and, as you can wash the cover in a washing machine on the wool cycle when needed, it is practical too.

Size
25 x 20cm (10 x 8in)

Materials
One 50g ball in A (black)
One 50g ball in B (white)
Suggested yarn: DK (worsted-weight); most machine-washable fibres will be suitable
40cm-long (16in) 4mm (US: 6) circular needle, plus one straight needle the same size for casting off
Stitch marker
Thin fleece fabric for the lining
Tapestry needle
One large snap button
Sewing machine to make lining (optional)
Sewing needle and thread

Tension
20 sts and 26 rows to 10cm (4in) square over st st using 4mm needles.

Pattern note
The iPad cover is knitted in the round, in one piece, starting from the ribbed section that will form the top opening. Finish the work by casting off using the three-needle method; this will form the bottom seam of the cover.

Make the iPad cover
With yarn A, cast on 88 sts. Join to work in the round, making sure not to twist the cast-on edge.
Place marker to indicate the start of the round and work in k1, p1 rib for four rounds.
Work the 62 rows of the chart (see p. 42).
When you have finished the chart, measure the cover to check that it is long enough for the iPad. If not, add rounds starting from round 54 and work for as many rounds as you need to achieve the correct length.
Cast off loosely using the three-needle method (see p. 102). Weave in any loose ends.

Make the lining
Fold the fleece fabric double. The fold will be the bottom of the lining bag. Measure 23cm (9in) along the fold and mark at each end. Measure 28cm (11in) for the length and cut out the lining. With a sewing machine, stitch the long sides together, 1cm (⅜in) from the edge. Alternatively, sew by hand using small backstitches. The RS will be on the inside. Turn the knitted cover inside out. By hand, stitch the corners of the

Chart for iPad cover

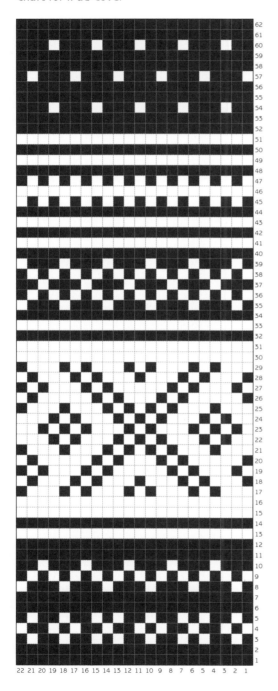

lining to the corners of the knitted cover. Make a few stitches in the middle of each edge, too. Turn the knitted cover over the lining and insert the iPad. Fold the top edge of the lining inwards so that it aligns with the edge of the knitted cover and sew it in place. By hand, stitch the lining and the cover together. Attach the snap button in the middle of the opening. (See p.108 for more detail.)

Head for a coffee shop with free WiFi, surf the internet and show off your creation!

Knitting through history

When I was growing up, I was sure that knitting was something we had always done in Norway. I later learned that knitting came to our shores in about 1800, or a little earlier.

I also thought we were the first people to knit, but I was wrong again. In Spain and Italy, people had been knitting fine silk stockings and nightshirts centuries before we knitted anything in Norway.

Once during a visit to Kew Gardens in London, I saw a shirt knitted in pineapple fibres from a South Pacific island! Knitting has been part of many cultures' history and it plays an important part even today. The convenience of synthetic fibres and cheap mass-produced clothing has not stopped us from knitting.

 = A

☐ = B

22-stitch pattern repeat
(work 4 times)

NECKTIE

A handknitted tie is a novelty these days, so why not make a special gift for a special man in your life? The combination of handknitting and a classic pattern means that this tie is not only a novelty but is also wearable. Try knitting it in red and white for a Christmas present.

The tie is knitted back and forth in rows and has an edging that is folded to the back of the tie to help keep it straight and flat. The rest of the tie is knitted in moss stitch.

Size
6.5cm (2½in) wide and about 150cm (59in) long

Materials
Two 50g balls in A (black)
One 50g ball in B (white)
Suggested yarn: DK (worsted-weight) wool
Pair of 3.5mm (US: 4) straight needles
Tapestry needle

Tension
27 sts and 28 rows to 10cm (4in) square over st st using 3.5mm needles.

Pattern note
The tie is made from the bottom up, so the decorative panel that will form the front of the tie is worked first. The tie is made with a bottom edge and side flaps that are turned back and sewn in place to give the tie some structure and firmness so that its holds it shape when worn.

Make the tie
With yarn A, cast on 19 sts.
Work four rows in st st.
Purl one row (on RS of work), then start working the chart (see p. 47) in st st.
At row 4, cast on 6 sts at the beg and end of the row. (31 sts)
The following rows are worked as follows: K5, p1, k19 (the pattern rows), p1, k5 on the RS, and p5, k1, p19, k1, p5 on the WS.
The edge sts will be folded to the back of the tie to prevent the edges from rolling up.

Work the edge sts as set above throughout the chart until you have completed row 56.

Shape the tie
Row 57: K5, p2, k17, p2, k5. (31 sts)
Row 58: P5, k1, p19, k1, p5.
Row 59: K5, p2, k17, p2, k5.
Row 60: P5, k1, p1, k1, p15, k1, p1, k1, p5.
Row 61: K5, p2, k1, p1, k13, p1, k1, p2, k5.
Row 62: P5, k1, p1, k1, p15, k1, p1, k1, p5.
Row 63: K5, p2, k1, p1, k13, p1, k1, p2, k5.
Row 64: P1, sl1, p1, psso, p2, (k1, p1) twice, k1, p11, (k1, p1) twice, k1, p2, p2tog, p1. (29 sts)
Row 65: K4, p2, k1, p1, k13, p1, k1, p2, k4.
Row 66: P2, sl1, p1, psso, (k1, p1) twice, k1, p11, (k1, p1) twice, k1, p2tog, p2. (27 sts)

Row 67: K3, p2, (k1, p1) twice, k9, (p1, k1) twice, k1, p2, k3.
Row 68: P1, sl1, p1, psso, (k1, p1) twice, k1, p11, k1, (p1, k1) twice, p2tog, p1. (25 sts)
Row 69: K2, p2, (k1, p1) twice, k9, (p1, k1) twice, p2, k2.
Row 70: Sl1, p1, psso, (k1, p1) three times, k1, p7, (k1, p1) three times, k1, p2tog. (23 sts)
Row 71: Sl1, k1, psso, (p1, k1) three times, p1, k5, (p1, k1) three times, p1, k2tog. (21 sts)
Row 72: (K1, p1) four times, k1, p3, (k1, p1) four times, k1.
Row 73: Sl1, p1, psso, (k1, p1) four times, k1, (p1, k1) four times, p2tog. (19 sts)

Cont in moss st for twelve rows. Dec 1 st at each end of the next and every 12th row until 15 sts rem.
Cont working in moss st over these 15 sts until the necktie measures about 150cm (59in).
Cast off and weave in any loose ends.

Finish the necktie
With an iron set on the 'wool' setting and using the steam function, carefully steam the necktie on the WS.
Fold in the edge sts and press carefully in place.
Note that if you press too much the texture will end up looking flat and lifeless.

With yarn A and a tapestry needle, stitch the edges neatly to the back of the tie.

New traditions
Knitted ties are often associated with casual wear and are not often seen in the office – that's what etiquette says, anyway. This knitted tie doesn't fall into the standard categories of knitted versus woven tie, so it is very much up to the owner to wear it as they like. I think it would look great worn with a plain shirt, a knitted cardigan and jeans! You could knit it in other colours and make it co-ordinate with a particular outfit. Whatever you do, you will be carrying a bit of knitting tradition into the future by wearing this tie!

Chart for necktie

■• p on RS, k on WS

□• p on RS, k on WS

■ = A

□ = B

▨ = no stitches

Chart shows whole of
patterned section

SLIPPERS

Treat your feet to a pair of cosy, warm slippers! The design looks a little like a pair of classic loafers, and the brioche-stitch sides make them thick and warm as well as stylish. The slippers would be a perfect weekend project and would make a great gift, too. Brioche stitch is easy to make and fun to knit. The slippers are knitted in two separate parts and the upper is stitched to the side and the sole.

Size	Small	Medium	Large
Length	23cm (9in)	24.5cm (9½in)	26cm (10¼in)

Materials
One[one:two] 50g balls in A (white)
One[two:two] 50g balls in B (black)
Suggested yarn: DK (worsted-weight) wool
Pair of 3.5mm (US: 4) straight needles
40cm-long (16in) 3.5mm (US: 4) circular needle
Tapestry needle

Tension
22 sts and 44 rows to 10cm (4in) square over garter st using 3.5mm needles.

How to work brioche stitch
Row 1 (set-up row): *Yo, sl1 as if to purl, k1, rep from * to end of row.
Row 2: *Yo, sl1 as if to purl, knit the yo from row 1 and the next st together, rep from * to end of row.
Rep row 2 until work measures desired length.

Note that the key to success when knitting brioche stitch lies in making sure that you knit the yarnover and the slipped stitch together.

To cast off, knit one row plain (knit the yo and the sl sts as one) and cast off on the next row.

Make the slippers
Make the upper part
With yarn A and straight needles, cast on 19[23:25] sts.
Knit eleven rows in garter st (knit every row) and then work the chart (see p. 51) as indicated for your size.
Note that the chart is worked in st st (k on RS and p on WS) and you start with a purl row.
Work the chart until row 46[50:54], then dec for the toe as follows on WS rows: P1, p2tog, p to last 3 sts, p2tog, p1.
Do this on every other row five times. (9[13:15] sts)
Cast off rem 9[13:15] sts.
Make the other upper part in the same way.

Make the sole

Start at the heel. With yarn B and straight needles, cast on 12[13:14] sts. Slip the first st on each row.

Knit all rows (to make garter st), and inc 1 st at the beg and end of every second row five times. (22[23:24] sts)

Knit until the work measures 20[21.5:23]cm (8:8½:9in). Dec at the beg and end of every second row four times. (14[15:16] sts)

Cast off.

Make the other sole in the same way.

Make the sides

With yarn A and the circular needle, pick up and knit 108[116:124] sts around the edge of the sole, starting at the middle back of the heel.

Making sure that the set-up row (row 1) is on the inside of the slipper, work back and forth in brioche stitch (see instructions on p. 49) until the side measures 3.5cm (1½in).

Knit one row with RS facing you.

Cast off loosely in purl.

Make the side of the other sole in the same way.

Finish the slippers

With yarn A and a tapestry needle, stitch the sides together at the back. Stitch the upper part onto the top edge of the side, starting at the toe so that you know the upper will be positioned symmetrically. Leave the garter-stitch part of the upper unstitched on both sides; this will stand up like a little tongue. Alternatively, you could fold it over the front of the slipper and attach it with a decorative button.

Weave in any loose ends.

Curl up on the sofa with a magazine and some warm slippers on your feet!

Chart for slippers

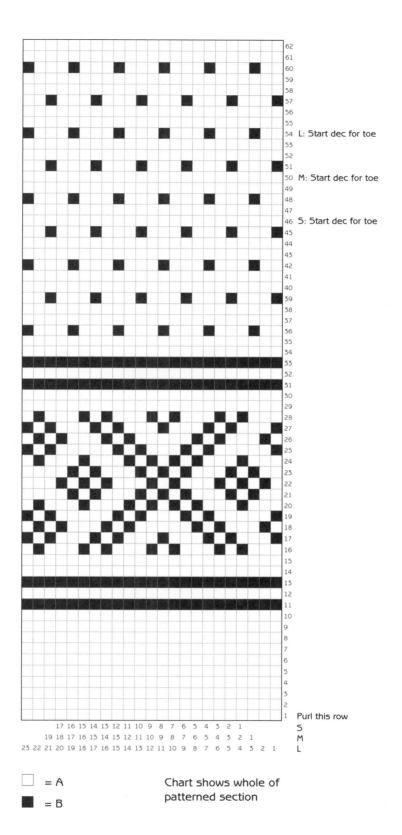

L: Start dec for toe

M: Start dec for toe

S: Start dec for toe

Purl this row

☐ = A

■ = B

Chart shows whole of
patterned section

WRISTWARMERS

It's nice to be outside on cold, clear days. Maybe you have plans for an autumn picnic or some spring clearing in the garden, or maybe you have naturally warm hands and find gloves to be too hot on winter days. That's when you will need these wristwarmers. They are knitted in two colours, which gives a comfortable double thickness. The Setesdal pattern combines well with most outerwear.

The wristwarmers are knitted on double-pointed needles from the wrist up to the fingers. The base of the thumb is made by increases as you knit, and the rib is knitted on to the thumb afterwards. If you feel the thumb is too tight when worked in ribbing, you can knit all the way and cast off in purl. To make a smaller size, try using smaller needles and finer yarn.

Size
28cm long x 11.5cm wide (11 x 4½in) when laid flat

Materials
One 50g ball in A (grey)
One 50g ball in B (cream)
Suggested yarn: DK (worsted-weight) wool
Set of 3.5mm (US: 4) double-pointed needles
Scrap yarn to use as stitch holder
Tapestry needle

Tension
25 sts and 30 rows to 10cm (4in) square over st st using 3.5mm needles.

Make the wristwarmers (make 2)
With yarn A, cast on 60 sts and divide over four needles (place 16, 14, 16 and 14 sts respectively on each needle).
Join to work in the round, making sure not to twist the cast-on edge as you do so.
Work six rounds in k2, p2 rib.
Start working the left wristwarmer chart (see p. 54) and work even until round 37.

Make the thumb
Round 38: M1, knit to end of round. The made st will be the middle of the thumb. Cont working the chart and make incs at each end of the thumb as indicated on rounds 39, 42, 45, 48, 51 and 54. (73 sts)
Rounds 55 and 56: K66 sts, place the next 15 sts on scrap yarn to hold for the thumb (last 6 sts of round 55, first 7 sts of round 56 and 2 sts from the hand). Cast on 2 sts and knit to the end of round 57. (60 sts)
Finish the chart and then work six rounds in k2, p2 rib.
Cast off loosely in patt.

Finish the thumb
Place the 15 sts from the scrap yarn back onto the needles.
Pick up the 2 sts you cast on at the beginning of round 57 plus the strand between the 2 cast-on sts. (18 sts)
Knit one round with yarn A.
With yarn A, work six rounds in k2, p2 rib.
Cast off in patt.
Knit the other wristwarmer in the same way, but this time work the right wristwarmer chart (see p. 55).

Finish the wristwarmers
With WS facing, weave in any loose ends. With an iron set on the 'wool' setting and using the steam function, gently press the wristwarmers.

Try them on and revel in the warmth of your own handiwork!

Chart for left wristwarmer

■ = A

□ = B

M = make 1 st

Chart shows whole piece

Chart for right wristwarmer

■ = A　　　　　Chart shows whole piece
□ = B
M = make 1 st

BEANIE HAT

My mother always used to tell me to wear a hat on cold days. As a teenager I thought that was very uncool. She argued that I only had one head and if I lost it, it wouldn't grow back, so wear your hat! I didn't lose my head, I wore my hat and now hats are in fashion too!

This hat combines fashion and tradition. The Setesdal pattern is one of the oldest knitting patterns in Norway, and it has given inspiration to countless designers worldwide. The main version shown here is in grey and cream, but I also made a red and cream colourway to give a more feminine look (see p. 59). I hope this design makes you feel inspired to try out your favourite colours.

Size
The hat is fairly stretchy, so one size should fit most people:
55–65cm (21¾–25½in) circumference; 21cm (8¼in) deep with the rib turned up (25cm/10in full length)

Materials
One 50g ball in A (grey)
One 50g ball in B (cream)
Suggested yarn: DK (worsted-weight) wool
40cm-long (16in) 3.5mm (US: 4) circular needle
Set of 3.5mm (US: 4) double-pointed needles
Stitch marker
Tapestry needle

Tension
25 sts and 30 rows to 10cm (4in) square over st st using 3.5mm needles.

Make the hat
With yarn A and the circular needle, cast on 132 sts. Join by working the first st on LHN with the working yarn from the RHN and being careful not to twist sts.
Place marker to indicate the start of the round and work in k1, p1 rib until piece measures 12cm (4¾in). Work the 45 rounds of the chart (see p. 59), shaping the crown when you have finished round 26 of the chart, as follows:

Shape the crown
Round 27: *K4, k2tog, rep from * to end of round. (110 sts)
Rounds 28–32: Knit, keeping bird's eye pattern correct.
Round 33: *K2, k2tog, rep from * to last st, k1. (83 sts)
Rounds 34–35: Knit.
Change to the double-pointed needles when you don't have enough stitches to fit comfortably around the circular needle.
Round 36: *K1, k2tog, rep from * to last 2 sts, k2. (56 sts)
Rounds 37–41: Knit.
Round 42: *K2tog, rep from * to end of round. (28 sts)
Round 43: Knit in B.
Round 44: Knit in A.
Round 45: K2tog in B to end of round. (14 sts)

Finish the hat
Break yarn, leaving a long tail about 30cm (12in). Thread yarn through rem sts and pull to gather the sts. Knot yarn tail securely on the WS. Weave in any loose ends.
With an iron set on the 'wool' setting and using the steam function, gently press the hat.

Wear your hat with pride, knowing that you look cool!

Choosing colours

When doing stranded knitting with two or three colours, it is relatively easy to change the colours to your preferred combination. There are a few things to keep in mind, however. I once knitted a cardigan in the Setesdal pattern using natural brown as the main colour and a traditional Faroe Island blue as the contrast colour. It looked nice while I knitted, but from a distance the blue disappeared and it looked bland. What had happened? When I was buying the yarn, I had held the two colours next to each other, and with equal amounts of both colours the contrast looked fine. However, with the main colour used in about 80 per cent of the cardigan and only a little of the contrast colour, the colours proved to be too alike in value, and the photo showed up grey without any visible pattern.

You can find out the value of colours by taking a black and white picture of them together. The value tells you how they look on a grey scale. When testing my cardigan, the brown and the blue turned out to have the same value. If you want to change the colours in a pattern, I recommend that you take a black and white picture of the yarn you want to use. If you can clearly distinguish the yarns by lighter and darker shades of grey, they should show up well in the finished design.

Chart for beanie hat

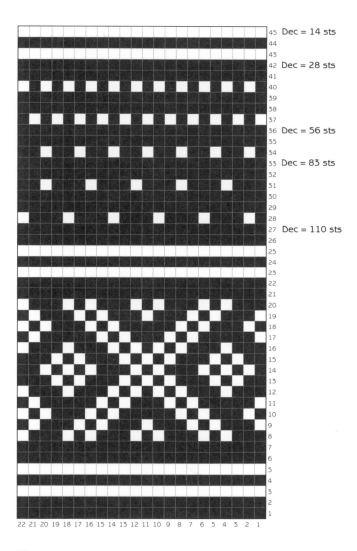

■ = A

□ = B

22-stitch repeat
(work 6 times)

FANA

BERET

You can never go wrong with a classic beret. Young girls and old men alike look sophisticated when wearing this great-looking headgear. The traditional Fana pattern lends itself beautifully to the shape of a beret. The rib is worked in two colours, and the check pattern usually found at the bottom of a Fana sweater is transformed into the rib. The beret is knitted from the headband up to the crown. You start out on a circular needle and then move onto double-pointed needles when you have fewer stitches to stretch around.

Size

Circumference will fit 50–58cm (19¾–22¾in) head

Materials

One 50g ball in A (duck egg blue)
One 50g ball in B (white)
Suggested yarn: DK (worsted-weight); most fibres with a bit of stretch will be suitable
40cm-long (16in) 3.5mm (US: 4) circular needle
Set of 3.5mm (US: 4) double-pointed needles
12 stitch markers
Tapestry needle

Tension

22 sts and 27 rows to 10cm (4in) square over st st using 3.5mm needles, before blocking.

Make the beret

With yarn A and the circular needle, cast on 126 sts and pm to indicate beg of round. Join to work in the round.
Work in rib as follows:
Rounds 1–3: *K3 in A, p3 in B, rep from * to end of round.
Rounds 4–6: *K3 in B, p3 in A, rep from * to end of round.
Rounds 7–9: Work as rounds 1–3.
With yarn A, knit one round; at the same time inc as follows: *K5, m1, rep from * to last 6 sts, k6. (150 sts)
Work chart 1 (see p. 64). The 12 sts of the pattern are repeated twelve times plus 6 sts.
Work chart 2 (see p. 64). Note that round 1 is an increase round, which you work as follows: *K10, m1, rep from * to end of round. (165 sts)
Work chart 3 (see p. 64). Note that the first round is a decrease round, which you work as follows:
*K5, k2tog, k6, k2tog, rep from * to last 8 sts, k8. (144 sts)
Keep working the chart. On round 18, place a stitch marker at every twelfth stitch. At round 20, dec after every marker by slipping 1 st, k2tog and passing the slipped st over the 2 sts knitted together. (120 sts)
Change to double-pointed needles when you have too few stitches to go around the circular needle.
Cont working the decs indicated on the chart until you have 24 sts left on the needles, then k2tog to dec throughout the next two rounds until you have 6 sts rem.
Break the yarn. With a tapestry needle, thread the yarn through the rem sts and pull tight. Pass the needle through the middle of the sts and secure the yarn on the WS.

Beret chart 1

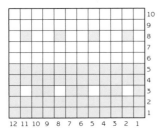

□ = A

□ = B

12-stitch repeat (work
12 times), plus 6 stitches

Beret chart 2

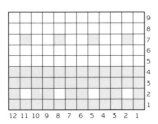

□ = A

□ = B

Make 1 st (m1) after
every 10 sts on round 1
for total of 165 sts

Beret chart 3

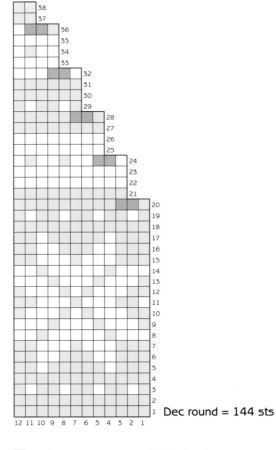

Dec round = 144 sts

□ = A

□ = B

▨ = decreased sts

Work the decreases
as indicated on the
chart and explained
on p. 63

Finish the beret

Weave in any loose ends and block the beret to achieve the
circular shape. To block the beret, first wet it thoroughly with
tepid water. Place a plate about 33cm (13in) in diameter
upside down inside the hat. Stretch the beret over the plate
so that the rim of the plate is positioned at the start of chart 3.
Leave the beret to dry at room temperature. Whenever you
wash the beret you will need to block it again so it retains
its shape.

Wear the beret out with your head held high!

HALF-SWEATER

Sometimes you just need a little extra something to keep you warm and snug. A thick sweater might be too much, and is big and bulky to carry around with you. Here is one solution that will turn heads – make just half a sweater! It folds up nicely without taking up too much space in your bag, and it looks stylish while keeping you warm. You get the effect of a whole sweater with one-third of the work! You don't even have to knit sleeves, although if you want to make separate ones, combine this top with the design on pp. 70–73.

The top is knitted in the round from the bottom up. It has shaped shoulders to make sure it stays in place and falls to around elbow-length. The length and shape emphasize the shoulders and make the waistline look slender. Who wouldn't like that?

Size	Small/ Medium	Medium/ Large
Width	100cm (39¼in)	114cm (45in)
Length	35cm (13¾in)	35cm (13¾in)

Materials

Three 50g balls in A (duck egg blue)
Three 50g balls in B (white)
Suggested yarn: DK (worsted-weight) wool
40cm-long (16in) and 120-cm long (48in)
  3.5mm (US: 4) circular needles
Two stitch markers
Two stitch holders (or scrap yarn)
Tapestry needle

Tension

27 sts and 33 rows to 10cm (4in) square over st st using 3.5mm needles.

Make the half-sweater

With yarn A and the longer circular needle, cast on 252[288] sts. Join by working the first st on the LHN with the working yarn from the RHN and being careful not to twist sts. Place marker at beg of round.
Work in k2, p2 rib for six rounds.
Start working the chart (see p. 68) and place the other marker at the opposite side of the work: K126[144] sts, pm, k126[144] sts.
Start dec for shoulder shaping on round 35 and work as follows:
K1, k2tog, k to 3 sts before marker, sl1, k1, psso, k1.
Rep on other side of marker. (248[284] sts)
Cont to work decs as indicated on chart. Keep the bird's eye pattern correct after the decs so that they are aligned above the one below.
Note that on round 74 you dec 2 sts on each side of the markers: K1, k3tog, k to 4 sts before marker, sl1, k2tog, psso, k1. Rep on other side of marker. (196[232] sts)
When you have worked the 76 rounds of the chart (192[228] sts), dec for
the shoulders as follows:

Shape the shoulders

Note that you will continue in the striped pattern throughout the top.
Leave 96[114] sts on a stitch holder for the back. You will now work back and forth in rows, knitting on the RS and purling on the WS.
Work the front:
Cast off 2 sts at beg of next four rows. (88[106] sts)
Cast off 4 sts at beg of next four rows. (72[90] sts)
Cast off 3 sts at beg of next two rows. (66[84] sts)
Place the sts on a stitch holder, and work the back in the same way.

Shape the neck

Knit all sts onto the shorter circular needle. (132[168] sts)
Place marker at beg of round and at 66[84] sts.
Working in the round, cont working the pattern according to the chart.
On round 88, dec as before at the markers. Cont to dec as indicated on the chart until you have 104[140] sts.
When you have completed round 94, work in rib as follows:
K1, *p2, k2, rep from * to last 3 sts, p2, k1.
Cont in rib for four rounds, then cast off loosely in patt.

Finish the half-sweater

With WS facing and tapestry needle threaded with matching yarn, sew the shoulder seams. Before breaking the yarn, make sure the RS looks neat. If not, undo the seam and sew again. Weave in any loose ends. With an iron set on 'steam' and a low temperature, press the top carefully. Make sure not to press down too hard, as this leaves the knitting looking flat and lifeless.

Try the half-sweater on and head for a mirror!

Chart for half-sweater

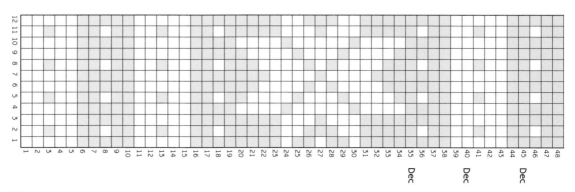

☐ = A

☐ = B

12-stitch repeat (work 21:24 times)

Dec = Decrease 1 st (or number indicated) on each side of markers

More style, less work

Making the half-sweater is actually less than half the job of knitting a whole sweater. There are other benefits to making this top, too. It is easy to pair with all sorts of outfits and works really well with jeans. I would love to go to a party in a stately home in the winter and dress in ice blue with this pulled over my shoulders. I would be an ice princess for a night!

Patterns that have been around for centuries do not disappear from knitting designs just because they are old; we find new ways to display the intricate beauty admired by generations of knitters and wearers. The half-sweater gives you a way to do just that.

Top

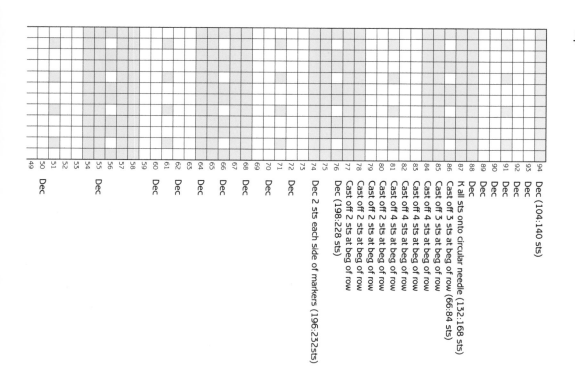

49
50 Dec
51
52
53
54 Dec
55
56
57
58
59 Dec
60
61
62 Dec
63
64 Dec
65
66 Dec
67
68 Dec
69
70 Dec
71
72 Dec
73
74 Dec 2 sts each side of markers (196:232sts)
75
76 Dec (198:228 sts)
77 Cast off 2 sts at beg of row
78 Cast off 2 sts at beg of row
79 Cast off 2 sts at beg of row
80 Cast off 2 sts at beg of row
81 Cast off 4 sts at beg of row
82 Cast off 4 sts at beg of row
83 Cast off 4 sts at beg of row
84 Cast off 4 sts at beg of row
85 Cast off 3 sts at beg of row
86 Cast off 3 sts at beg of row (66:84 sts)
87 K all sts onto circular needle (152:168 sts)
88 Dec
89 Dec
90 Dec
91 Dec
92 Dec
93 Dec
94 Dec (104:140 sts)

SLEEVES

Sometimes a sweater is too much and a T-shirt too little to feel comfortable. Then is the time to take inspiration from professional cyclists! These sleeves are inspired by cyclists' armwarmers, but given a special Norwegian twist. If you are a cyclist or a long-distance runner, you can put these pretty sleeves to good practical use. If you are not, wear the sleeves with a T-shirt and jeans or combine them with the half-sweater on pp. 66–69, and just look stylish! These sleeves are easy to knit and you can play around to find fun outfits to wear them with.

Skill level
easy

Size

42cm (16½in) long; 28cm (11in)
circumference at top

Materials

Two 50g balls in A (duck egg blue)
Two 50g balls in B (white)
Suggested yarn: DK (worsted-weight) wool
Set of 3.5mm (US: 4) double-pointed
  needles
Stitch marker
Tapestry needle

Tension

25 sts and 31 rows to 10cm (4in) square
over st st using 3.5mm needles.

Pattern note

You start working the sleeves at the narrower end for the wrist,
and then gradually increase so the sleeve will fit around the
broader part of your arm and over your elbow.

Make the sleeves

With yarn A, cast on 48 sts (place 12 sts on each needle).
Join to work in the round, making sure not to twist the cast-on
edge as you do so. Pm to mark beg of round
Work in k2, p2 rib for six rounds.

Start working chart 1 (see p. 72).
When you have completed the 15 rounds of the chart, start
working chart 2 (see p. 72) and inc 1 st at the beg and end of
the first round as follows: K1, m1, k to last st, m1, k1. (50 sts)
Then inc as indicated on every tenth round.
Rep chart 2 seven times (you will have seven yarn B stripes).
(64 sts)
Note that the pattern will not match at the end of some of the
rounds due to the increases. Work the increased sts into the
pattern as you go along.
If you want to make longer sleeves, add further chart 2 rounds
before starting chart 3.
Work chart 3 (see p. 72), making sure to keep the bird's eye
pattern correct as you start the chart. You might have to start
at a different point in the chart to get the bird's eyes to fit on
the same line. As indicated on the chart, inc 1 st at the beg
and end of rounds 23 (66 sts) and 29 (68 sts), working the
incs as follows: K1, m1, k to last st, m1, k1.

When you have worked chart 3, work five rounds in k2, p2 rib.
Cast off loosely and check that the cast-off edge is elastic
enough to sit comfortably at the top of the arm. If it is too
tight, undo it and cast off more loosely.

Finish the sleeves

Weave in any loose ends. Gently press the sleeves with an iron
set on the 'wool' setting and using the steam function. You
might want to stretch the sleeves both lengthways and
widthways if the work looks a bit uneven. Sometimes this
happens when you knit with double-pointed needles; a little
stretching might help.

If you are off to your Tour de France practice on a cold day, you
will turn some heads among your teammates. If not, you might
end up turning some heads with these cool sleeves anyway!

Sleeves chart 1

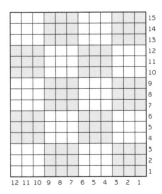

15
14
13
12
11
10
9
8
7
6
5
4
3
2
1

12 11 10 9 8 7 6 5 4 3 2 1

▨ = A

☐ = B

12-stitch repeat
(work 4 times)

Sleeves chart 2

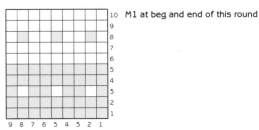

10 M1 at beg and end of this round
9
8
7
6
5
4
3
2
1

9 8 7 6 5 4 3 2 1

▨ = A

☐ = B

M1 = make 1 st

Sleeves chart 3

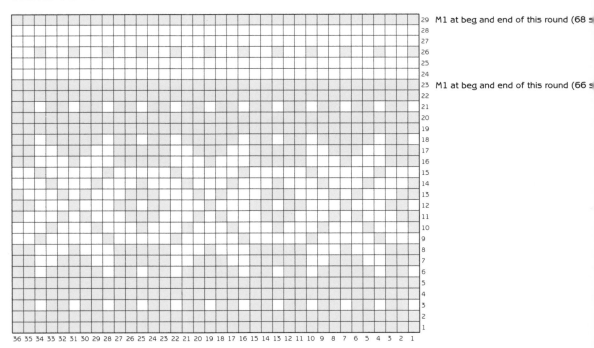

29 M1 at beg and end of this round (68 s
28
27
26
25
24
23 M1 at beg and end of this round (66 s
22
21
20
19
18
17
16
15
14
13
12
11
10
9
8
7
6
5
4
3
2
1

36 35 34 33 32 31 30 29 28 27 26 25 24 23 22 21 20 19 18 17 16 15 14 13 12 11 10 9 8 7 6 5 4 3 2 1

▨ = A

☐ = B

M1 = make 1 st

CAFETIÈRE COSY

This beautiful coffee-maker cosy will keep your coffee warm for longer, and will do so in style! The traditional colours of the Fana pattern – duck egg blue and white – will lend a lovely touch of colour to your kitchen. The Fana design has a clean and contemporary look and will make any gatherings around your coffee table even nicer! Colourwork is perfect for keeping items warm, as the strands on the wrong side create a double thickness to the knitted fabric. This cosy will fit a standard six-cup coffee-maker or cafetière. It is kept in place by three clear snap buttons along the side.

Size
Fits a standard-size cafetière: cosy measures 30cm (12in) wide, 14cm (5½in) high

Materials
One 50g ball in A (duck egg blue)
One 50g ball in B (white)
Suggested yarn: DK (worsted-weight); most
  fibres will be suitable but wool is ideal
Pair of 3.5mm (US: 4) straight needles
Tapestry needle
Three small clear plastic snap buttons
Sewing needle and thread

Tension
24 sts and 32 rows to 10cm (4in) square
over st st using 3.5mm needles.

Make the cosy
With yarn A, cast on 80 sts and work back and forth in k1, p1 rib for five rows.
Start working the chart. Note that the first 4 sts and the last 4 sts of each row are knitted in k1, p1 rib in yarn A. When you work rows in yarn B, remember to carry yarn A with you on the WS so you can work the edges in A. The best way to carry the yarn is to twist the yarn that you carry with the main colour you are working with after every 3 sts.
When you have finished working the chart, work in k1, p1 rib for four rows.
Cast off in patt, not too loosely.

Finish the cosy
Weave in any loose ends. Gently press the cosy with an iron set on a low temperature and the steam function on. Do not press too hard as this will take the springiness out of the wool. Attach the snap buttons to the edge stitches, one at each end (above and below the handle) and one in the middle of the cosy. Make sure that one half of the snap button is placed on the WS of the cosy and the other on the RS. That way they will not show when the cosy is attached to the cafetière.

Enjoy a cup of coffee with friends and family!

Chart for cafetière cosy

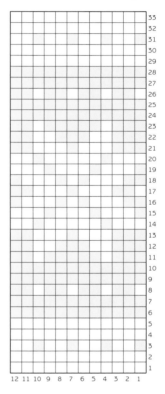

☐ = A

☐ = B

12-stitch repeat (work 6 times), plus 4 lots of k1, p1 rib sts at beg and end of each row

CUP COSIES

Whether you pick up a coffee to go or you use a tall glass to serve tea, these cup cosies will keep your fingers safe from scalding and keep your drink warm! They are inspired by the patterns of the Fana sweater. Each of the variations shows off one of the three pattern elements that make up the sweater: the rose, the stripes and the checks. You can match the cup cosies with the cafetière cosy on pp. 74–75; you could also try making them in different colourways to suit your kitchen décor.

The cup cosies are knitted from the bottom up on double-pointed needles. It might feel cumbersome to knit small items like these on double-pointed needles, but take it slow and easy to start with and it will feel much easier once you have completed the first few rounds.

Size
The cosies are approximately 12cm (4¾in) high and will fit a cup or glass about 14cm (5½in) tall with a circumference of 27cm (10½in) at the top. The cosy is stretchy and will easily fit somewhat bigger cups. If you want it to fit a smaller cup, try knitting with smaller needles (such as 3mm).

Materials
One 50g ball in A (duck egg blue)
One 50g ball in B (white)
Suggested yarn: DK (worsted-weight) wool
Set of 3.5mm (US: 4) double-pointed
  needles
Stitch marker
Tapestry needle

Tension
24 sts and 32 rows to 10cm (4in) square over st st using 3.5mm needles.

Make the cosies
With yarn A, cast on 54 sts (place 13, 14, 13 and 14 sts respectively on each needle). Join to work in the round, making sure not to twist the cast-on edge as you do so. Pm to mark beg of round.
Work four rounds in k1, p1 rib.
Start working the chart for the cosy design of your choice (see three options on p. 78).
Inc 1 st where indicated on the chart. When all the incs are made, you will have 58 sts.
Note that the pattern will not match at the end of every round, so work the increased st in the colour that fits the pattern best. It is easy to see which colour the increase should be made in; in design 2 it is indicated on rows 8 and 18 which colour you should use to make the increases.
When you have finished the chart, knit one round in yarn A followed by three rounds in k1, p1 rib. Cast off loosely in patt.

Finish the cosies
Weave in any loose ends on the WS.

Make yourself a big cup of coffee!

Cosy design 1

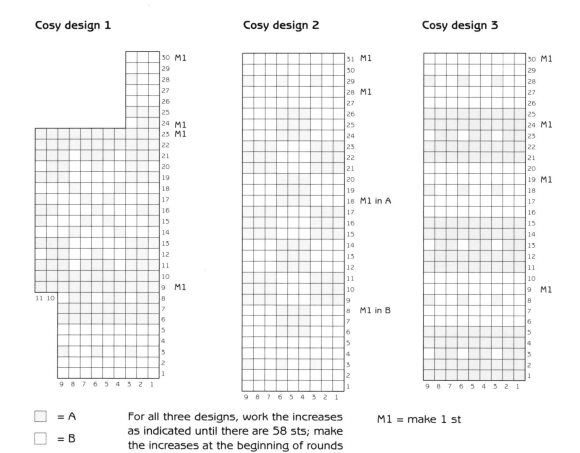

Cosy design 2

Cosy design 3

☐ = A

☐ = B

For all three designs, work the increases as indicated until there are 58 sts; make the increases at the beginning of rounds

M1 = make 1 st

Knitted cosies

For years, knitted cosies were limited to hot water bottles, teapots and eggs. The creativity of knitters has extended the range to include computers, coffee mugs and wine bottles, just to mention a few. There are really no limits to what you can cover in knitting. I have seen chair leg cosies that double as floor protectors, as well as camera cosies and flowerpot cosies. Take a look around you and see if there is anything that could benefit from a knitted cover!

VOSS

TOILET ROLL COVER

This retro-style toilet roll cover is a really fun project to make. I remember toilet roll covers from my childhood, and I must admit that they are not one of the bathroom textiles I have much nostalgia for. However, this is a fun and quirky item, and reminds us how much things change, even in our bathrooms. No one these days is offended by seeing the next toilet roll in line standing naked on the shelf, but I think it's time to put that idle toilet roll to good use and cover it with some beautiful handicraft! This classic design will also give a quick facelift to the smallest room in the home and would make a great quirky gift, too.

Skill level
easy

Size

Fits a standard toilet roll (10cm/4in high)

Materials

One 50g ball in A (grey)
One 50g ball in B (white)
Suggested yarn: DK (worsted-weight); most
  smooth-fibred yarns will be suitable
Set of 3mm (US: 2/3) double-pointed
  needles
Stitch marker
Tapestry needle

Tension

26 sts and 32 rows to 10cm (4in) square
over st st using 3mm needles.

Make the toilet roll cover

With yarn A, cast on 80 sts (20 sts on each needle). Join to
work in the round, taking care not to twist the cast-on edge.
Pm to mark beg of round.
Work k2, p2 rib for four rounds. Knit one round.
Start working the chart. When you have completed the chart,
cont to work in yarn A and dec for the top as follows:
*K8, k2tog, rep from * to end of round. (72 sts) Knit 1 round.
*K7, k2tog, rep from * to end of round. (64 sts) Knit 1 round.
*K6, k2tog, rep from * to end of round. (56 sts) Knit 1 round.
*K5, k2tog, rep from * to end of round. (48 sts) Knit 1 round.
*K4, k2tog, rep from * to end of round. (40 sts) Knit 1 round
*K3, k2tog, rep from * to end of round. (32 sts) Knit 1 round.
*K2, k2tog, rep from * to end of round. (24 sts) Knit 1 round.
*K1, k2tog, rep from * to end of round. (16 sts). Knit 1 round.
Next round: K2tog to end of round. (8 sts)

Finish the toilet roll cover

Break the yarn about 35cm (14in) from the work. Thread a
tapestry needle with the end of the yarn and thread through
the rem 8 sts. Pull tight and secure the thread on the WS of
the work. Weave in any loose ends.

Cover the toilet-roll-in-waiting and cast on for the next one!

Chart for toilet roll cover

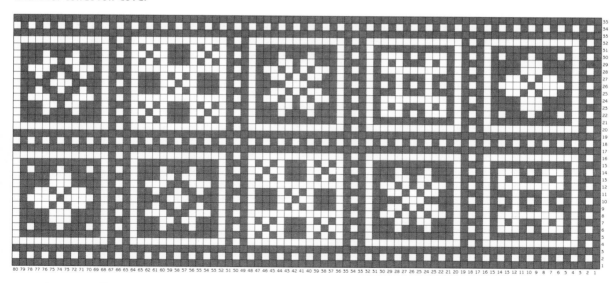

■ = A   Chart shows whole piece
□ = B

POTHOLDERS

Potholders are one of the bare necessities in a kitchen. We reach for them every time we cook, often with our focus on whether the food has turned out as we hoped. Potholders might be a bit overlooked, but they are still essential items. Knit these potholders to brighten up your kitchen; the geometric Voss pattern looks great in many different colour combinations, and since they are quick to knit you can always have a pair to hand in the most fashionable kitchen colours! Here I have made them in complementary colourways.

Skill level
easy

Size

22 x 22cm (8¾ x 8¾in)

Materials

(Enough to make two potholders)
Three 50g balls in A (grey)
Three 50g balls in B (white)
Suggested yarn: 4ply (sport-weight) cotton
40cm-long (16in) 4.5mm (US: 7) circular
    needle, plus one straight needle the
    same size for casting off
Stitch marker
Tapestry needle

Tension

20 sts and 22 rows to 10cm (4in) square
over st st using 4.5mm needles with yarn
held double.

Make the potholders

With yarn A held double, cast on 96 sts.
Join to work in the round, making sure not to twist the cast-on
edge as you do so. Pm to mark beg of round.
Knit two rounds.
Work the chart and then knit two more rounds in yarn A.
Cast off using the three-needle method (see p. 102).
Knit the other potholder in the same way, but swapping the
colours around.

Finish the potholders

With the yarn held double, finger crochet a length of 20 chain
(see p. 104). Attach the length to one corner of the potholder
to form a loop. Secure the yarn ends on the WS. Weave in any
loose ends. Stitch together the cast-on edge and take care
that the pattern matches on both sides.

Enjoy cooking!

Chart for potholder

■ = A
□ = B

Chart shows one
complete side; repeat
for other side

SNOOD

A loose-fitting and snug snood is like a good hug. It is not bulky like a scarf, but sits nicely around your neck to keep out chills on a cold and windy day. You can knit the snood in different types of yarn: cotton will make a snood that falls nicely at the base of the neck, while a snood knitted in wool will be warm and firm. If you want a touch of luxury, try a cashmere yarn or a fuzzy mohair yarn.

Skill level
easy

Size
26 x 28cm (10½ x 11in) when laid flat

Materials
Two 50g balls in A (white)
One 50g ball in B (olive green)
Suggested yarn: DK (worsted-weight)
    cotton/merino blend
40cm-long (16in) 4mm (US: 6) circular
    needle
Stitch marker
Tapestry needle

Tension
23 sts and 24 rows to 10cm (4in) square
over st st using 4mm needles.

Make the snood
With yarn A, cast on 128 sts.
Join to work in the round, making sure not to twist the cast-on edge as you do so.
Place stitch marker at beg of round. Work k2, p2 rib for six rounds.
Start working the chart. Once the chart is complete, work five rounds in k2, p2 rib in yarn A and then cast off loosely. Try to get the elasticity of the cast-off edge as close as possible to that of the cast-on edge. Weave in any loose ends.

Finish the snood
With an iron set on the 'wool' setting and using the steam function, gently press the snood. Make sure not to press too hard or the material will look flat and the stitches squashed.

Pop the snood over your head and check yourself out!

Chart for snood

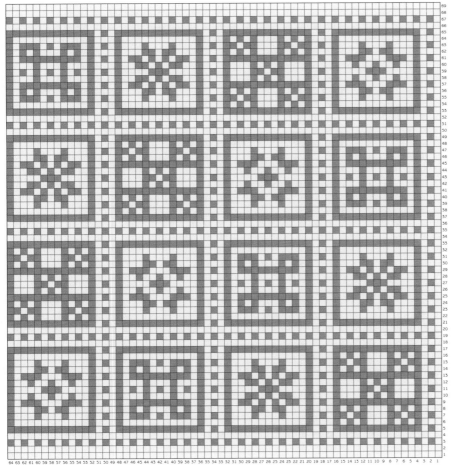

□ = A
■ = B

Chart shows one
complete side; repeat
for other side

CUSHION COVER

A handknitted cushion cover will give a really snug and cosy feeling to a room. This cover is knitted in the traditional Voss pattern, a geometric look that blends well with many contemporary home-furnishing styles. Thick needles and chunky yarn make this a fast and fun project. You could easily knit up a pair of cushions over a rainy weekend! There is no end to the colour combinations you can try out; play around to find the colours that fit your personal style.

Size
50 x 50cm (19¾ x 19¾in)

Materials
Three 50g balls in A (beige)
Three 50g balls in B (white)
Suggested yarn: super chunky (super bulky weight) wool
60cm-long (24in) 7mm (US: 10½) circular needle, plus one straight needle the same size for casting off
Four 21mm (¾in) snap buttons
Stitch marker
Tapestry needle .
Cushion pad to fit the cover

Tension
13 sts and 15 rows to 10cm (4in) square over st st using 7mm needles.

Make the cushion
With yarn A, cast on 134 sts and join to work in the round. Make sure not to twist the cast-on sts as you do so. Pm to mark beg of round.
Knit five rounds, purl one round and then knit two rounds.
Work the 66 rounds of the chart (see p. 90).
When you have finished working the chart, cast off using the three-needle method (see p. 102).

Finish the cushion
Weave in any loose ends.
Fold the first five knitted rounds to the inside of the cushion cover at the purl round. With an iron set on the 'wool' setting and the steam function on, very gently press the cushion cover, taking care that the pattern matches on both sides. With yarn A and a tapestry needle, stitch the turned-in edge in place on the inside of the cover. Stitch on the snap buttons evenly spaced apart.

Insert the cushion pad, place the cushion on the sofa and take a brief nap to test it out!

Chart for cushion cover

■ = A
☐ = B

Chart shows one complete side;
repeat for other side

Make your own traditions

As with all the traditional knitting patterns of Norway, there are many varieties and interpretations around. When women's magazines that included knitting patterns became readily available in the late 1940s, standardization began. I have seen lots of varieties on the Voss pattern: some have the same motif in all the squares; some have the squares set up like a brick wall; others have broken lines between the squares. Looking at the old sweaters, it's as if they are saying 'there are no rules'.

The squares that build up the Voss pattern make this a particularly good design for cushions, blankets and other cosy accents in your home. In a way the pattern is a little like Lego pieces: you can build your own patterns from the squares and shift the motifs around as you like.

IPHONE COVER

There are lots of great-looking covers you can buy for your phone, but why not make something unique yourself? Mobile phones are such an important part of our lives that you may as well make your phone's home personal. This little project is also a great way to get rid of scrap yarn and put leftovers to good use. It will knit up in no time at all and would also make a lovely gift for a friend. The geometric Voss pattern invites you to play with different colour combinations; if you want to try out a particular colour choice before you make a bigger project, this would make a good trial run.

Skill level
easy

Size
The cover fits an iPhone and other phones the same size or smaller. It is approximately 13.5 x 6.5cm (5½ x 2½in)

Materials
One 50g ball in A (cream)
One 50g ball in B (dark red)
Suggested yarn: 4ply (sport-weight); most
  fibres will be suitable
Set of 3.5mm (US: 4) double-pointed
  needles
Stitch marker
Tapestry needle

Tension
26 sts and 30 rows to 10cm (4in) square over st st using 3.5mm needles.

Pattern note
The cover is knitted from the opening down. Swap the colours around if you prefer.

Make the iPhone cover
With yarn A, cast on 32 sts (8 sts on each needle). Join to work in the round, making sure not to twist the cast-on edge. Pm to mark beg of round.
Work k2, p2 rib for five rounds.
Start working the chart.
When you have finished the chart, divide the sts between two needles (16 sts on each) and turn the work inside out. Make sure you have the pattern centred on the back and the front so that st 1 starts one needle and st 17 the other. Cast off using the three-needle method (see p. 102).

Weave in any loose ends and turn the cover RS out again.

Tuck your phone in!

Chart for iPhone cover

□ = A   Chart shows whole piece
■ = B

TECHNIQUES

KNITTING IN THE ROUND

Many of the projects in this book are knitted in the round; generally, smaller-scale projects such as the iPhone cover and the toilet roll cover are made on double-pointed needles (dpns), whereas larger projects such as the racerback top and the cushion cover are made on a circular needle. I like to use a circular needle whenever there are enough stitches to fit comfortably around the needle. In addition, with some projects (such as the beanie hat), you will start on a circular needle and switch to dpns when there are too few stitches to fit comfortably around the circular needle.

Casting on with double-pointed needles

There are two ways to cast on when you are knitting with a set of double-pointed needles. You can start by casting on the correct number of stitches on each of the needles you are going to work with. For example, if you are going to cast on 40 sts, you cast on 10 sts on each of four needles. The other way is to cast on all the stitches on one needle and transfer the correct number to the other needles you are going to use.

All projects using double-pointed needles in this book are knitted on a set of five needles, where you hold stitches on four needles and knit with the fifth.

When you join to knit in the round, take a look at the cast-on edge to make sure it is straight and not twisted. If it is twisted, you will have to unravel the work and start again. There is no easy way out of it! My experience is that if something feels wrong when you knit, it probably is. So double-check to see whether the cast-on edge is twisted – you might not notice it until you have worked a few rounds.

As you work along, make sure you know where the end and start of the round is. It can be useful to take a piece of scrap yarn in a contrasting colour and weave it in as you knit: after every five or ten rounds just slip the thread between the last and first stitches of the round. Since the thread is passed loose between stitches, you can easily pull it out when you have finished the work.

The first few rounds can be a little tricky on double-pointed needles. Don't give up; it is the same for everybody, even the most experienced knitters, and it will start to feel much easier after a few rounds!

Double-pointed needles are ideal for knitting smaller-scale projects in the round. Don't worry if it feels fiddly at first – work slowly and concentrate on not twisting your stitches.

Casting on with a circular needle

It is easy to cast on with a circular needle: you simply cast on all the stitches you need and then start knitting. Make sure the cast-on edge is not twisted before you begin.

It is the same as with double-pointed needles; it might take a few rounds before you notice and the only way to solve the problem is to unravel the work.

When you knit in the round on circular needles, use a stitch marker to indicate where the round starts. Slip the marker onto the needle between the last stitch of the worked round and the first stitch of the round you are about to work. As you knit along, you slip the marker so it always remains in place to indicate where the round ends and starts.

Types of knitting needles

Knitting needles come in a variety of materials, including plastic, metal, bamboo and wood. No one type is better than another and every knitter will have their own preferences. I find that wood and bamboo needles make less noise if you knit in a public place, and particularly if you knit on a set of double-pointed needles. Knitting needles are tools and the important thing is that you find out what works best for you.

STRANDED KNITTING

There are two main reasons for stranded knitting in traditional Norwegian knitting: the first is to achieve beautiful patterns and adorn the garment; the second is to make warm sweaters, mittens and hats. The result of stranded knitting is that you have a double layer of yarn. Where one colour of yarn shows at the front of the sweater, the other is on the inside and adds insulation.

There are a few things you need to be aware of if you are new to stranded knitting.

Knitting with two colours
Norwegian patterns are created by knitting with two colours: one background colour and one pattern colour. The colour not in use is carried across the wrong side of the work. The yarn at the back of the work forms a strand when it is not used for knitting. Stranded knitting is easier than you might think if you are new to it. The most important thing to have in mind when you knit with two colours is that the elasticity and tension of the work should be the same as if you were knitting with just one colour.

There are two potential pitfalls in stranded knitting: pulling the strand at the back of the work too tight, or leaving it too loose.

To avoid pulling the yarn too tight when you change colour, stretch the work on the right-hand needle (the stitches you have just worked) a little after changing colour (after you have knitted the first stitch in the other colour). This adjusts the strand to the elasticity of the work.

To avoid having strands hanging too loosely at the back of the work, pull a bit tight when you change the colour and stretch the work to make sure the strand is in line with the row.

If you are new to stranded knitting, it might take a bit of practice to get it right. I encourage you not to give up if you find it difficult. Everyone can master it, including you. It opens up many possibilities to knitting fun things.

Wrapping the strand

In Norwegian knitting, the change of colours appears at quite short intervals. You will notice that it is quite common to have three stitches between changes of colour, although sometimes the yarn at the back has to be carried for longer stretches of stitches. To avoid the strand forming a long, loose loop at the back of the work, you will need to wrap the strand with the yarn you are working with.

For example, if you have a stretch of five stitches, knit three stitches, then twist the working yarn with the yarn you carry at the back once, then knit two stitches. I normally wrap the strand at every third stitch. By doing this I retain a good tension to the work and avoid ending up with long strands that can easily snag when the work is finished.

If you feel you need some extra guidance with this technique, there are a lot of helpful videos on the internet. Another nice way to gain confidence with stranded knitting is to join a knitting club and learn from knitters in a social setting.

One main benefit of stranded knitting is that the resulting double layer creates extra insulation – ideal for cold-weather accessories such as these Setesdal wristwarmers.

This is the wrong side of the Voss cushion cover, with the strands of the two working yarns visible.

WORKING FROM CHARTS

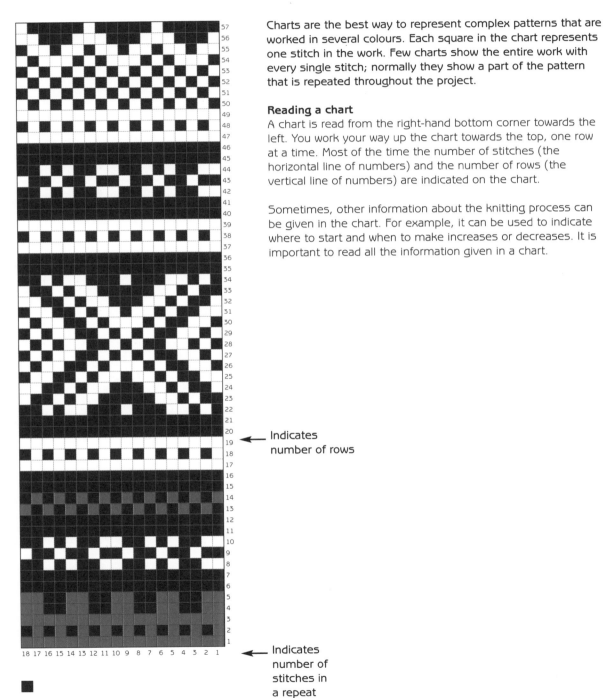

Charts are the best way to represent complex patterns that are worked in several colours. Each square in the chart represents one stitch in the work. Few charts show the entire work with every single stitch; normally they show a part of the pattern that is repeated throughout the project.

Reading a chart

A chart is read from the right-hand bottom corner towards the left. You work your way up the chart towards the top, one row at a time. Most of the time the number of stitches (the horizontal line of numbers) and the number of rows (the vertical line of numbers) are indicated on the chart.

Sometimes, other information about the knitting process can be given in the chart. For example, it can be used to indicate where to start and when to make increases or decreases. It is important to read all the information given in a chart.

← Indicates number of rows

← Indicates number of stitches in a repeat

← Colour key

Adding colours

When you do stranded knitting and add a new colour, just take the yarn and let a 15–20cm (6–8in) tail hang at the back of the work. The first stitch will be very loose, but you will pull this tighter when you weave in the loose ends at the end of the project. When you are working from a chart and you see you do not need one of the colours any more, cut it at about 15–20cm (6–8in) from the work. It is the same with the last stitch of a colour as with the first; it will be loose, but you can tighten it when weaving in ends during the finishing process.

Changing colourways

You can always change the suggested colourway of a project. If you feel restrained by the colours in the chart, take a black and white photograph of it and let your creativity do the rest! Make sure there is enough contrast between the colours you choose so that they show up clearly in relation to each other.

Altering the size

If you want to alter the size of a project based on a chart, you can easily do it! It is easiest with pattern charts that are based on repeats, like most of the projects in this book. If you want the pattern to make full repeats and achieve an unbroken pattern all the way along the project, you need to add one complete pattern repeat. So for an 18-stitch pattern repeat, you will need to add 18, 36 or 54 stitches (multiples of 18) until you achieve the size you want.

To be sure how many centimetres you are adding, you can check the tension. If 23 sts equals 10cm, you can then calculate that 2.3 sts equals about 1cm; hence you are adding about 8cm to the project by adding one pattern repeat of 18 stitches. (The calculation: 23 divided by 10 = 2.3, hence 2.3 sts per centimetre. Then add 2.3 with itself until you get close to the number of stitches you are adding: $2.3 \times 8 = 18.4$. Hence you add a bit more than 8cm.)

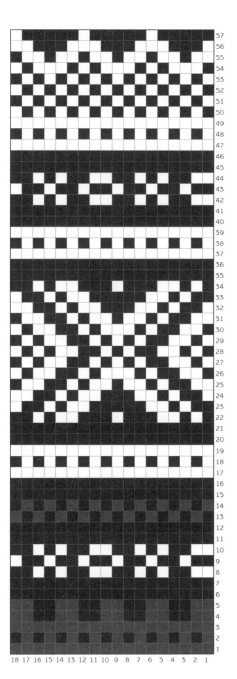

Making a black and white copy of a chart is useful if you want to change the colours in a project.

SPECIALIST FINISHING TECHNIQUES

A number of the projects in this book feature finishing techniques with which you might not be familiar. It is worth trying these out, as they will add a really professional-looking finish to your piece.

The three-needle cast-off creates a good solid seam for items that need to retain their shape.

Three-needle cast-off

This casting-off method is used in a couple of the projects, including the Setesdal iPad cover and the Voss cushion cover. It creates a very clean, crisp edge that is useful for retaining the shape of rectangular and square-shaped items.

Casting off using the three-needle method is not very different from ordinary casting off; the main difference is that you have stitches on two needles rather than just one. In a three-needle cast-off, you will have the same number of stitches on each of the two needles.

Hold together the two needles containing the stitches to be cast off, with the tips facing the same way. Insert a third needle through the first stitch on both needles and knit them together. It is like knitting two stitches together, but here the two stitches sit on different needles. Knit the next two stitches together and pass the first stitch over in the same way you would with an ordinary cast-off. Continue until all stitches are cast off.

Kitchener stitch/grafting

The straps of the racerback top are joined using Kitchener stitch (also known as grafting). This creates a seamless join that will be pretty much invisible. I use this for shoulder seams, sock toes and any other seam that I want to be invisible.

Grafting involves joining two sets of stitches that are still on their needles. Hence it replaces casting off and stitching the pieces together afterwards. Using a tapestry needle threaded with the yarn that was used to knit your project, you sew a row of stitches that looks exactly like knitting. In this book grafting is done in stocking stitch only.

You will have the same number of stitches on each needle. Hold the needles parallel, with the wrong sides of the knitting together and the right sides facing outwards.

Thread a tapestry needle with the loose yarn end of the project, and start the set-up.

Insert the threaded tapestry needle into the first stitch on the knitting needle closest to you as if to purl and pull it through, leaving the stitch on the needle.

Then insert the tapestry needle into the first stitch on the back knitting needle as if to knit, leaving the stitch on the needle. Pull the yarn through.

The set-up is complete. Then repeat the following four steps until all stitches are off the needles:

1 Insert the needle into the first stitch on the front needle as if to knit, then slip it off the end of the needle.
2 Insert the needle into the next stitch on the front needle as if to purl, but leave it on the needle. Gently pull the yarn through.
3 Insert the needle into the first stitch on the back needle as if to purl, and slip it off the end of the needle.
4 Insert the needle into the next stitch on the back needle as if to knit, and leave it on the needle. Pull the yarn through.

When all the stitches are off the needles, tighten up the sewn stitches to match the tension of the other knitted stitches. You can use the tapestry needle to tug at each loose loop in turn.

I recite a little chant in my head when I graft stitches; it makes it easier to remember the four steps:

Set-up:
1 Front, purl, on
2 Back, knit, on

Grafting:
1 Front, knit, off
2 Front, purl, on
3 Back, purl, off
4 Back, knit, on

Front/back refers to the knitting needle, knit/purl refers to the way you insert the tapestry needle and on/off to what you do with the stitch you just worked through.

The straps of the racerback top are grafted together to create an invisible join on the right side.

Double crochet edging

Double crochet (known as single crochet in the US) is a good way to create a neat finish on knitted edges such as arm openings or necklines, without adding a rib. In this book I used it around the neckline and armholes of the racerback top.

With the yarn used for the project and a crochet hook in the given size, insert the hook into a stitch on the very edge of the knitted project. Catch the yarn with the hook and pull it through the stitch. Insert the hook into the next stitch along the edge, catch the yarn and pull it back through the stitch again. Now you have two loops on the hook.

1 Catch the yarn and pull it through both loops on the hook to complete one double crochet stitch.
2 Insert the hook into the next stitch along the edge of the knitted project, catch the yarn and pull it back through.

Repeat steps 1 and 2 until you have crocheted around the entire edge. Then insert the hook in the crocheted stitch you made first, catch the yarn and pull it back through the stitch. Catch the yarn once more and pull it through the loop on the hook. Cut the yarn and pull it through the loop.

When you work your way around an arm opening, stop from time to time and check the tension. If you feel the edge is too loose, undo the stitches and start again, tightening your stitches more after each one you work. If you feel the crochet edge is too tight, undo it and do not tighten your stitches as much. Alternatively, you could pick up more stitches along the knitted edge.

Finger crochet

Finger crochet is used to make the hanging loops for the Christmas stocking and the potholders.

1 Create a slipknot approximately 15cm (6in) from the end of the yarn. Insert your index finger and thumb through the slipknot.
2 Grasp the long length of yarn (the one attached to the ball of yarn) with your index finger and thumb. Pull this yarn with your index finger and thumb through the slipknot. With your other hand, pull the short end of yarn to tighten the stitch. The yarn you pulled through has now formed a new loop. Continue pulling the yarn through the loop on your finger and thumb and pull the short end to tighten the crocheted string. When you have the desired length, cut the yarn and pull it through the loop.

Finger crochet is a simple and neat way to create a hanging loop.

Embroidering teddy bear Maurice's face

Teddy bear Maurice's face is embroidered in the main colour (blue) using a tapestry needle.

Start with the eyes: make a slipknot about 20cm (8in) from the end of the yarn. Position the first eye at the same height as the top of the snout and about 3 stitches out. Insert the needle through 1 stitch (one stitch forms a V) and pass the yarn through the loop of the slipknot. Pull tight. Stitch a cross over the knot and make sure not to make it bigger than the knitted stitch, unless you want bigger eyes.

After you have made the last part of the cross, bring the needle out where you want to position the other eye. Pull the yarn a little bit to get a very small indent where the eye is. Keep the yarn tight and make a knot stitch (after you have passed the thread around the back of 1 stitch on the bear's head, pass the needle through the loop formed and pull tight) around the stitch where you are making the eye. Make a cross over the knot stitch and fasten. With the needle still inside the head after the last part of the cross, bring it out where you want the nose to be.

I placed the top horizontal of the nose about 3 stitches down from the top of the snout and made it about 3 stitches wide, which leaves 1 stitch between the decrease/increase rows on each side. The nose should be centred on the middle row of stitches (the one that starts at the top of the snout). Make a few more horizontal stitches, each shorter than the previous one, to make a triangular-shaped nose.

Now, still following the middle row of stitches, make two short backstitches to form the slit from the nose to the mouth. Each stitch should be about 5mm (¼in) long. At the bottom of the slit, make a stitch to one side that covers about 2 stitches. Bring the needle out about 2 stitches across on the mouth and make another stitch from the outer side towards the middle of the mouth. Bring the needle out again in the blue stitches at the neck and fasten the yarn with a knot stitch in the strand between two knitted stitches.

Pull tight, insert the needle through the teddy and pull out the yarn at the back of the neck. Cut the yarn close to the body and pull at the knitted fabric to make the loose end of the yarn disappear inside the teddy.

I gave Maurice a faint smile; you can give your teddy the expression you want him or her to have!

Teddy bear Maurice's facial features in full embroidered detail!

GENERAL FINISHING TECHNIQUES

Once you have finished making your piece, it is worth spending extra care and effort over the finishing processes, such as blocking the piece into shape and sewing up the seams neatly.

Sewing up seams

When sewing seams in handknitted fabric, you can work with the stitches that are there to join them in a neat way. Grafting (see p. 102) leaves no evidence of stitching together, but if you have to sew up side seams you need a different method.

Before you start sewing up your pieces, it is advisable to block them. I use an iron set on 'wool' with the steam function on for this process (see below). This helps to control any rolling at the edge of stocking-stitch pieces.

Use a tapestry needle and the main yarn used for your project. Pin the two pieces together, as this will make it easier to hold the two parts in place. Use mattress stitches, working with the right side of both pieces facing you. Pass the needle under the strand between two stitches on the edge of the knitted piece. (Each knit stitch looks like a V and there is a strand between the Vs). Make sure you retain the elasticity of the knitted project and do not pull the sewing too tight.

Pressing and blocking

Knitted items are naturally elastic, which means it is possible to manipulate their shape. When you work in stocking stitch, the edge has a tendency to roll; this can be reduced by blocking and pressing.

Many people block a knitted item by stretching it into position when damp, pinning it to a surface and leaving it to dry. I normally use an iron. Set it on the 'wool' setting with the steam function on. Very gently press the project; do not press down too hard or the knitted surface will be squashed flat and look lifeless. If you happen to do this by mistake, washing the item should help to revive it.

With the Fana beret, blocking is done by placing a dinner plate inside the crown while the beret is damp.

Some items are not pressed at all, like Maurice the teddy bear (although if you find you want to press it before stuffing the body, that is fine). If you feel your knitting has an uneven surface, a light pressing and some gentle tugging might help to even out the stitches.

Blocking will help to set your knitted
items into their desired shape.
A dinner plate is used to block
the Fana beret.

Aftercare

If you want to prolong the life of your knitted item, you will
need to take care when washing it. Some types of yarn can be
machine-washed, but it is generally safest to hand-wash your
knitting gently.

There are some general rules to stick to:

Wool should in general be hand-washed in tepid water using
mild detergent. You should avoid agitating or twisting the item
as you wash it; wool felts very easily and you do not want that
to happen to something you have made.

Never dry wool in a tumble dryer. Whatever you put in will
come out much smaller and harder, and there is nothing you
can do to repair the damage!

Cotton does not felt and can go in the washing machine, while
some handknit cotton yarn can be tumble-dried.

Whatever type of yarn you use, check the ball band of the yarn
for any care or washing instructions.

General finishing techniques

LININGS AND FASTENINGS

Sometimes you will want to line your knitted project. In this book the iPad cover is lined; you could line the iPhone cover and the cushion cover too. There are a few things to consider when you want to line a knitted project, the main one being whether it needs to keep its elasticity. This is true for the iPad cover and the iPhone cover, but not for the cushion.

I added a fleece lining to the Setesdal iPad cover.

Lining items that need to keep their elasticity

Make sure you use a lining material that has some elasticity, such as fleece fabric or jersey. Fold the fabric double with the right sides together facing inwards. Place the item that will go inside the knitted project on the lining fabric. Place the bottom of the item in line with the fold in the fabric and trace around the item with chalk or a pen. Cut out the lining about 2cm (¾in) from the traced line. With a sewing machine, sew up the sides of the lining, leaving the top open. You could do this by hand instead, using small backstitches.

Turn the knitted item inside out and sew the corners of the lining to the corners of the knitted item with a few stitches. Turn the knitted item back over the lining. You now have the lining inside the knitted item. Make sure the lining is tucked properly into the knitted item. Use a pin to hold the bottom of the lining and the knitted item together. Now fold the top of the lining inwards (towards the inside of the knitted cover). Make sure the folded edge of the lining lines up with the knitted edge, or is slightly shorter (5mm/¼in or so). Stitch in place using a thread of a similar colour to the outer knitted cover.

Lining items where the lining does not need to be elastic

If you want to line a cushion or other item that does not need to be elastic, follow the instructions above, but note that in this case you do not need to use elastic fabric; you can use woven fabric such as cotton or purpose-made lining fabric.

Adding fastenings

When you attach snap buttons to knitted fabric, you can use a sewing needle and sewing thread of a similar colour to the main colour of your knitted project. If you are attaching large buttons, you can use knitting yarn and a tapestry needle. Check to see that the tapestry needle can fit through the holes in the buttons. If the needle fits easily, you can use the knitting yarn.

When you sew on buttons, make sure to work through each hole several times and secure the threads on the back of the work so the buttons do not come loose.

Snap fastenings are added to the cafetière cosy to make it easy to remove.

ABBREVIATIONS

beg	beginning
cm	centimetre(s)
cont	continue
dec(s)	decrease(s)
DK	double knit
dpn(s)	double-pointed needle(s)
g	gram(s)
in	inch(es)
inc(s)	increase(s)
k	knit
k2tog	knit two stitches together (decrease by one stitch)
k3tog	knit three stitches together (decrease by two stitches)
LHN	left-hand needle
m1	make one (increase by one stitch)
mm	millimetre(s)
p	purl
p2tog	purl two stitches together (decrease by one stitch)
patt	pattern
pm	place marker
psso	pass the slipped stitch over
rem	remain(ing)
rep	repeat
RHN	right-hand needle
RS	right side
sl	slip
st(s)	stitch(es)
st st	stocking stitch
tog	together
WS	wrong side
yo	yarnover
*	repeat the pattern instructions from * the number of times stated
()	repeat the pattern instructions contained within the brackets the number of times stated
[]	used to divide instructions and stitch counts in patterns with multiple sizes

CONVERSIONS

Knitting needle sizes

In this book we have used metric needle sizes; if you use US needle sizes, here is a handy conversion chart to refer to.

Metric size	US size
3mm	–
3.25mm	3
3.5mm	4
3.75mm	5
4mm	6
4.5mm	7
5mm	8
5.5mm	9
6mm	10
6.5mm	10½
7mm	–
7.5mm	–
8mm	11
9mm	13
10mm	15

Crochet hook sizes

As with knitting needles, the US has its own idiosyncratic sizing system for crochet hooks. Here is a conversion chart for common sizes.

Metric size	US size
3.25mm	D3
3.5mm	E4
3.75mm	F5
4mm	G6
4.5mm	7
5mm	H8
5.5mm	I9
6mm	J10

European and American knitting and crochet terms

Sometimes stitches and technical terms are called different things in Europe and the US. Here is a quick guide.

European terms	US terms
cast off	bind off
double crochet (dc)	single crochet (sc)
tension	gauge
moss stitch	seed stitch
stocking stitch (st st)	stockinette stitch (st st)

ACKNOWLEDGEMENTS

I owe my joy and interest in knitting to my upbringing: my mother taught me how to knit, and always kept the house full of yarn. Along with my two creative sisters, I had plenty of company when we played with yarn and needles, be it knitting, crochet or tapestry.

I had many helpers on the journey towards developing the patterns in this book. I must thank Juliet Bernard for many things, but most of all for her generosity and willingness to share her contacts and knowledge.

Working with Anova Books has been a joy. Commissioning Editor Amy Christian's professional and efficient way of working has suited me well, and she is a pleasure to work with. The team at the photo shoot – photographer Fiona Kennedy, her assistant Kate Davis, Amy Christian and designer Zoe Anspach – all deserve thanks for being so pleasant and professional to work with. Nicola Hodgson has put in a lot of work to make sure that all the knitting patterns are easy to follow, and her keen eye for good writing has been invaluable. The book shows how good they all are!

At home in Oslo, Norway, I would like to thank my husband Arve for mustering up an interest in knitting that is not really there. He has been a surprisingly good discussion partner on all aspects of knitting and pattern designing. He has been patient and supportive all the time his home was overflowing with yarn, knitting needles and charts.

Last but not least, I would like to thank my friends who contributed to the development of many of the designs in this book. As the starting point was 'sweater patterns – but no sweaters', many dinner table conversations circled around what sort of patterns I could make. So many creative ideas were brought to the table, and some have been rejected. The rejected ideas created much laughter, though!

First published in the United Kingdom in 2013 by
Collins & Brown
10 Southcombe Street
London
W14 0RA

An imprint of Anova Books Company Ltd

Copyright © Collins & Brown 2013
Text and pattern/project copyright © Eline Oftedal 2013

ISBN 978-1-90844-9-474

A CIP catalogue record for this book is available from the British Library.

10 9 8 7 6 5 4 3 2 1

Reproduction by Mission, Hong Kong
Printed by 1010 Printing International Ltd, China

This book can be ordered direct from the publisher at www.anovabooks.com

Photography by Fiona Kennedy
Additional picture credits: Eline Oftedal p6, 7, 79. Christina Wilson p8. Scanpix /NTB /Jan Nordby p9, /Privat p10, /Kno.NTB p11 /NTB arkib p12. iStockphoto/SiriGronskar p37.

Join our crafting community at LoveCrafts – we look forward to meeting you!